Osbournes

CONFIDENTIAL

Osbournes
CONFIDENTIAL
AN INSIDER'S CHRONICLE

MICK WALL

BOOKS

First published in Great Britain in 2008 by
JR Books, 10 Greenland Street, London NW1 0ND
www.jrbooks.com

A catalogue record for this book is available from the British Library.

ISBN 978-1-906217-73-0

1 3 5 7 9 10 8 6 4 2

Printed by MPG Books, Bodmin, Cornwall

Plate section: page 1 © Corbis; page 2, 3, 6 © Rex Features; page 4, 5, 7 8 © Getty Images

This book is dedicated to
Linda Mary, Evelyn Rose, Mollie Diana and
Michael Joseph – always.

Acknowledgements

The author would like to thank the following people:
Linda Wall, Robert Kirby and Jeremy Robson, absolutely without whom...

Also, *Classic Rock, Mojo, Kerrang!, The Mail On Sunday*, Radio One, BBC2 and all the other media outlets that provided the excuses over the years for me to spend as much time as possible with Sharon and Ozzy. Also Lynn Seager, David Arden and Ross Halfin, I haven't forgotten. Also Don Arden, still Mr Big.

And of course, to Ozzy and Sharon personally, for always being you. My love and thanks – always.

Act 1

In Which Our Hero, the Prince of Darkness
Is Assailed by All & Sundry, Only to be Rescued
By the Lady Sharon, Daughter of Don,
Overlord of the Rock Underworld

Scene One:

A Nice Sunday Lie In

In the long, hot summer of 1985 I had been hired to write Ozzy Osbourne's official biography. There was nothing special about my appointment; it wasn't like they had gone out and sought the best man for the job. Nor was I the first man for the job. There had already been at least three previous attempts made by other writers to get the job done. The first go at it, bizarre as it seems now, had been by Alastair Campbell, future New Labour spin doctor and attack dog, then overseer of the *Daily Mirror*'s pop page. Ozzy's verdict: 'Load of fucking rubbish!' At least, that's what he told me, though it's possible that he may not have actually read it, books not being something Ozzy usually 'did'. Second and third versions by various others had met with similar fates, though why exactly was never made clear to me. 'I can't remember why we didn't like them,' said Sharon, Ozzy's wife and manager. 'I think they were just boring.' Blimey, I thought, they must have been bad if they made Ozzy Osbourne's life story sound boring.

Why they then turned to me, though, was much easier to fathom. I just happened to be the person labelled 'writer' standing nearest at the moment they decided they needed one. Lately, Ozzy and I had become close. That is, we had gotten drunk together a few times; occasions which I was then able to turn into stories for various newspapers and magazines. Hard to imagine now, I suppose, but back then any journalist willing to hang out with Ozzy and write – mainly positive – stories about him was rare enough to be regarded as an official friend of the family.

The other bonus for them in employing me, I knew, was that I never made any great demands on Ozzy or Sharon when doing these stories. There might be the occasional switching on of a tape recorder, but not so as Ozzy would have noticed. Mainly, I just needed to share the same oxygen as him for a few hours and I would have everything any journalist could want, Ozzy – and Sharon, though she wasn't famous enough yet to warrant inclusion in the finished articles – being brilliantly adept at providing funny stories, wacky incidents and general tales of ordinary madness without the prompt of some boring writer's even more boring questions.

More than any other rock star – or indeed any other person – I had ever come across Ozzy was just one of those people that lit up any room he was in. He may not have been much of a singer, but as a frontman he was formidable, by turn uproariously jolly and, next, bottom-of-the-well melancholy, both onstage and off. And of course he liked a drink, and taking drugs, though it was always the drink far more than the drugs he could not do without. Subsequently, there was always something going on whenever Ozzy Osbourne hit town. From biting the heads off bats to shaving off all his hair, retiring, coming back, retiring again and coming back again, often in the space of a week, to being fired from his own band, to watching his guitarist die in a light aircraft accident, to being arrested for urinating on the

Alamo while dressed as his wife, to standing there straight-faced as he told the nice middle-aged lady with the fixed smile from the TV news crew how the first song he was going to sing onstage at Live Aid was 'Food Glorious Food'…you didn't need to interview Ozzy to have something to put in your story, you just needed to be there to see what happened next.

Writing a book about him though…that was going to need something a tad more substantial, surely? A proper interview, for a start. At least one, in fact. Probably. The only problem was that every time we scheduled a 'proper' sit-down face-to-face interview something always seemed to go wrong. First Ozzy was out of town when he was supposed to be in town; then he was in town when he was supposed to be out but 'busy'. One time, I turned up at his London office for a pre-arranged meeting just as he was leaving. 'Oh, I didn't think you were going to turn up,' he said, by way of some sort of explanation. Then jumped in his car and was gone again. Another time, I turned up at the large mansion house in London he and Sharon were then renting in Berkeley Square only to find them both in bed together with the flu. I sat on the end of the four-poster bed while Ozzy farted loudly beneath the duvet, blamed Sharon, who turned round and hit him, then asked me to open a window, but we still didn't get our interview done. Then there were the times I turned up somewhere on the road and he was either too drunk to talk or simply too stunned at being sober. These were the days, you see, when Ozzy was either very much on the wagon – or totally off it. There never was any middle ground with Ozzy. It was one of the big reasons why those of us who put up with the fucker loved him so. And why he drove us all mad.

Finally, to make up for all the trouble he had put me to, he said,

Ozzy offered to cook us Sunday lunch, after which he promised we would get down to the business of putting his precious recollections on tape. I had assumed that when he said he would cook lunch he meant he would get the cook to cook lunch but when I dutifully turned up again at the house in Berkeley Square one sunny Sunday afternoon in August and Sharon showed me into the kitchen, I was greeted by the surreal sight of Ozzy actually standing at the sink with his flowery pinafore on, peeling potatoes.

'Er, can I help?' I asked. 'No, no,' he shook his head, 'All under control.' I grabbed a seat at the table and watched him fussing over the roast beef in the oven. In the hallway outside I could hear Sharon – then heavily pregnant with the boy they would call Jack – and the nanny busying themselves with the children – Aimee, nearly three, and Kelly, nearly two – getting ready to go out to play in Hyde Park while Daddy finished making them all lunch. As the front door closed behind them, Ozzy froze in his tracks – literally, turned into a statue. I thought he might be having a seizure or something.

'Everything all right, Ozzy?' I asked.

'Shut up....'

I did as I was told, watching him standing there, his eyes as big and frightened as a deer's, nose twitching, antlers raised, ears alerted by the snap of a twig beneath the hunter's boot. I listened with him to the sound of footsteps retreating up the garden path, the swinging open and closing again of the squeaky front gate. We carried on silently listening as the sound of car doors slamming shut came to us, followed by the noise of an ignition being turned over. We carried on listening in absolute silence – I wasn't sure to what exactly – as the car slowly drove off, Ozzy still not moving a muscle, his whole being tuned to the sounds of Sharon's retreat. As the sounds of the car finally faded, to be replaced by the sound of the now boiling spuds bubbling over, he exhaled hugely.

'Thank fuck for that,' he sighed. 'Do you wanna drink?'

I didn't know what to say. Ozzy was then supposed to be 'on' the wagon and I didn't want to get the blame from Sharon for being the one that had caused him to fall off – again. Before I could say anything though, he had yanked open the large refrigerator door and pulled out a cold bottle of white wine, of which there appeared to be a stack on the top shelf; something French and expensive-looking. He looked in the drawer for a corkscrew, couldn't find one – or not quickly enough – lost patience and just pushed his thumb down on the cork until it slid with an inverted pop into the wine bottle. Then he grabbed two pint beer glasses and emptied the contents of the bottle into them. He shoved one of the pint-glasses in my hand, two-thirds full of white wine and tiny bits of cork.

'Cheers!' he cried, downing his own pint-glass of wine in one long, ungraceful haul, the wine spilling down his chin onto his pinny. 'Fucking hell, I needed that!' he gasped as he set down the empty glass with a loud thud. 'Do you fancy another?' I had barely started on my own pint of wine but Ozzy yanked another bottle from the refrigerator, applied the clearly practised thumb and poured most of the contents into his glass and a little top-up into mine. Down in one it went again. I began to fret. What would Sharon say when she got back and found him – us – like this? I had a glug from my own pint glass and thought about it.

'What's Sharon going to say when she sees you've – we've – been drinking?' I asked gingerly.

'Fuck it,' he said. 'I'll tell her you made me.'

I chuckled nervously. A joke, it must be. But he wasn't laughing.

Instead he was working the cork down into another bottle, the sweat of concentration dripping from his nose....

The meal itself was a memorable affair. Ozzy had laden the table with roast beef, Yorkshire pudding, gravy, cabbage, carrots and peas, and a large bowl of mashed potato smothered with melted cheese and garnished with parsley and thin slices of tomato. We filled our plates – Sharon, the nanny, the kids and I. Sharon filled Ozzy's plate for him as he didn't seem able to manage it. I don't know how many pint-glasses of wine he had put down by the time Sharon and the kids arrived home but I was onto my second, which meant he was probably onto his sixth or seventh.

To my astonishment, Sharon hadn't batted an eye, just taken one look at her husband, then at me, clocked what was going on and without a word went back to getting the children ready for lunch. We all sat at the large table in the dining room, bedecked with fresh flowers, sparkling silver cutlery and large, pleasingly clunky cream-coloured crockery sitting on a crisp white tablecloth. Sunlight streamed through the tall bay windows looking out onto the pretty back garden. Despite the fact that Ozzy, whose enunciation – the result of a braying Brummy accent flecked with Los Angelino and sanded down by years of drugs and alcohol – was slurred even at the best of times, was now apparently beyond speech, lunch had begun pleasantly, everyone chatting at once, the children all smiles and silly jokes, Sharon very much the proud indulgent mother sitting at the head of the table doing her best to deflect attention away from the impending disaster seated next to her.

Then, about five minutes into the meal, the light in Ozzy's eyes blinked out and his head very gently lowered itself onto his plate until it came to rest in the peas and potatoes. Ozzy began to snore, the gravy bubbling noisily around his nose, his long blond hair – as it still was then – nestling onto the plate. Nobody said anything. We just carried on as normal, passing the peas over his head and making small talk. As I was sitting opposite I couldn't help but stare directly at him, face down in his food, and felt it rude not to at least pass some comment.

'Um…I think Ozzy's fallen asleep,' I said.

Sharon glanced over at him, as if noticing her unconscious husband for the first time, then went back to her meal, saying something pleasant to one of the children.

'Um…is he all right?' I wondered out loud to no one in particular.

'Fuck him!' Sharon barked at me. Then, smiling sweetly, 'Pass the gravy please, darling….'

We sat and ate our lunch, passing dishes over his head while Ozzy lay with his face in his plate, snoring. When the meal was over, Sharon and the nanny had just begun clearing away the plates when Ozzy finally came to. Raising his head from his plate as slowly as he'd lowered it half an hour before, he looked around and gave out the call now familiar to millions of TV viewers the world over: 'Shaaaaaron!!!'

'What?' she snapped.

'Help!'

'Why? What have you done now?'

He looked down at himself. The large stain on his pinny, the mash falling from his face and hair, the cold lumpy gravy smeared across his face.

'I'm all fucked-up…'

'And whose fault is that?'

He looked like he was going to cry. 'Shaaaaron…please…help meeeee…'

She stood there looking at him, not with contempt or even much real anger. It was more…tedium. Like she had seen this all before so many times, which, I realised suddenly, she must have. Ozzy tried to stand but couldn't make it and found himself collapsing back onto the table, scattering plates everywhere. Sharon shook her head wearily. 'Fuck's sake', she sighed. Then she grabbed him by the arm, yanked it around her shoulders and helped him stagger out the door and up the stairs to bed. I sat there, fingering my pint of wine with the bits of cork floating in it, wondering if I was ever going to get my interview done, whether the bloody book would ever be written. And even if it was, what it was I was supposed to write. Not the truth, obviously.…

When Sharon returned a short while later it was like nothing had happened. As if we'd just returned from a pleasant trip round the garden admiring the roses, perhaps. She looked at me and, smiling sweetly, nodded towards my nearly empty pint-glass and asked: 'Would you like a proper glass for that?'

'Thank you,' I said, 'That would be very nice.'

Sharon fetched me a proper wine glass, a new bottle of very good red, opened it with a very fancy-looking corkscrew and poured me a fresh drink. Then we sat down by the fireplace. Still no mention of Ozzy's state or what – or who – had caused it.

'Right,' she said, 'you better get out your tape recorder. We'll be waiting forever for that fucker to talk to you. Whatever you want to know, you better ask me. Where did you want to start?'

Act 1
Scene Two:

Ninety Thousand Dollars and Told to Fuck Off

The first time I met Ozzy had been at a party in London in 1979 – and, no, it wasn't like a scene from *The Osbournes*. Or rather, it was, except there was only one famous Osbourne back then and nobody was laughing at him – not to his face anyway. So miserable was Ozzy, in fact, that it threatened to put a damper on the occasion: a stag party for one of the musicians I worked for as a PR back then: Jimmy Bain, former bassist with Deep Purple offshoot band Rainbow, now fronting his own Thin Lizzy offshoot outfit, Wild Horses and soon to become more successful as a sideman in Black Sabbath offshoots, Dio. (Not forgetting that Lizzy, Purple and Sabbath were themselves offshoots of other, previous outfits – hey, welcome to the wacky, backslapping global village known as seventies hard rock and heavy metal!)

Any party involving people like that in those days would naturally have meant lashings of whisky, cocaine, marijuana, amphetamines and heroin, but as this was officially a stag party and therefore a cut above the norm you could now add strippers performing simulated sex acts to the mix – or 'stimulated sex acts' as Jimmy's honoured guest, Thin Lizzy singer Phil Lynott put it. And because you can't have sex and drugs without at least a smidgen of rock'n'roll, the whole thing was being held in a large rehearsal room in north London where along one wall a stage had been set up so that the various musicians could get up and – hey now! – jam at some suitably shit-faced point in the never-ending evening.

So far, so: what a wonderful night in 1979. Then Ozzy arrived and the mood in the room shifted. Ozzy had 'left' Black Sabbath earlier that year – that is to say, been booted out – and word was he'd been on a non-stop bender ever since, an impression his dishevelled appearance that night did nothing to dispel. Hunched over and dazed-looking, accompanied by two minders who led him around the room like some prize exhibit he appeared to be on autopilot, the words already tumbling out of his mouth before I had finished introducing myself.

'Ninety thousand dollars I was given and told to fuck off,' he said as I shook his limp, sweaty hand. I gathered he was talking about his recent sacking from Sabbath. 'Left to fucking die, I was.' He stared right through me. 'I mean, what you would do?' I noticed he was drooling. Before I could formulate some sort of reply, he was off again, blabbering at the next outstretched hand. '…Ninety thousand dollars…told to fuck off…' I watched him waddle away, his minders grinning inanely.

For me, though, this was no joke. Although it was no longer acceptable to say so in the restrictive post-punk mien of the late-seventies, I had once been a Black Sabbath fan. Seeing their singer wandering around like a ghost at his own funeral was something I could not have imagined back in the days when, in a prolific frenzy spanning just three years (1970–73), Ozzy and Sabbath had released the five albums that would forge their legend, becoming the benchmark by which every subsequent generation of 'heavy' rock artists would be forced to measure up to. As Metallica drummer Lars Ulrich once told me, 'Without Black Sabbath there simply wouldn't have been a Metallica.' Like their contemporaries, Led Zeppelin, Ozzy and Sabbath's influence would eventually seep like blood through a bandage into other, less obvious areas of the musical landscape, too. Kurt Cobain once described Nirvana as 'a cross between Black Sabbath and The Beatles'; the Red Hot Chili Peppers memorably drew heavily on the riff to 'Sweet Leaf' (from Sabbath's 1971 *Master Of Reality* album) for their 1992 breakthrough hit, 'Give It Away'; while future-shock rock artists like Marilyn Manson and Henry Rollins, and hip hop stars like Ice T, Busta Rhymes and even the late Ol' Dirty Bastard would all eulogise Sabbath on stage, in print and even occasionally on record. And that was all long before *The Osbournes* came along and turned reality TV into Big Business, making everybody forget that Ozzy had once been the singer in a really great band.

Yes, folks, it's true. Once upon a time, the name Ozzy Osbourne was synonymous with something more than just swear words, forced laughter and a family so clearly dysfunctional they make the Addams Family look like the Brady Bunch; something so entirely different in fact, something so subversive and dark, it's almost impossible to believe now. For in an era when it seemed possible to measure a band's musical prowess by how 'heavy' they were, they didn't come any weightier than Black Sabbath. There were, it's probably fair to

13

say, 'none more black'. And, despite only having one recognisable hit single – 'Paranoid', No. 3 in the UK, in August 1970 – there were even fewer more successful.

A four-piece formed from the ashes of two locally well-known groups called The Rare Breed and Mythology, all four founding members of the original Black Sabbath – vocalist John Michael 'Ozzy' Osbourne (b. 3 December 1948), guitarist Frank Anthony 'Tony' Iommi (b. 19 February 1948), bassist Terence Michael Joseph 'Geezer' Butler (b. 17 July 1949) and drummer William 'Bill' Ward (b. 5 May 1948) – grew up within half a mile of each other, in the same narrow, grey streets of Aston, a tiny Birmingham suburb then struggling to come to terms with the mess Hitler's bombs had made of it. With the exception of Iommi, who was an only child, they all came from large, working class families. And though they all shared a deep love of music – The Beatles for Ozzy, the Mothers Of Invention for Geezer, the Shadows and Chet Atkins for Iommi, and a combination of all of the above plus drum-titans Joe Morello and Gene Krupa for Ward – they all saw the opportunity to form a successful group, Ozzy would later tell me, 'as the quickest way out of the fucking slums.'

Along with a bottleneck player called Jimmy Phillips and a sax player who may or may not have been called Lou Clarke (none of them can remember), Black Sabbath had actually begun as a six-piece, in the summer of 1968, under the name The Polka Tulk Blues Company – a name Ozzy filched, he told me, from 'a Paki shop in Handsworth.' Their first three gigs – a caravan site in Cumbria, and two nights at a ballroom in Carlisle – 'were a fucking disaster', Geezer recalled. So Iommi – 'who always cracked the whip' – sacked the other guitarist and sax player and the band started again as a four-piece called The Earth Blues Company – a mouthful quickly shortened to Earth. Over the next few months Ozzy and Earth began to make a name for themselves on the same local Midlands circuit that had already spawned acts like Carl Wayne & The Vikings (who later became The Move, before splintering yet again, in the seventies, into Roy Wood's Wizzard and Jeff Lynne's Electric Light Orchestra); Deep Feeling (featuring Jim Capaldi, Dave Mason and Stevie Winwood, all later of Traffic); and future Led Zeppelin star Robert Plant's Listen (which also featured Zeppelin drummer John Bonham).

Still relying mainly on covers and 'extended jams' whenever they scored a spot at cooler dives like Henry's Blueshouse or The Penthouse, the turning point for Earth came with the first original number they wrote together, a doleful piece of 'psychedelic blues' Geezer called 'Black Sabbath' – an enigmatic title lifted from the 1963 Boris Karloff film of the same name (aka *Black Christmas* and/or *Three Faces of Fear*). The maudlin, knife-quivering chords that Iommi repeats throughout were actually based on the opening stanza to 'Mars' from Holst's *The Planets*. 'I loved "Mars",' explained Geezer, 'and I was playing it on me bass one day [hums lumbering, dramatic opening] and Tony just changed it around slightly and it just seemed to write itself from there.' Ozzy improvised the lyrics around a nightmare-experience that Geezer had related to him. 'Cos like, I was getting into black magic and the occult and all that kind of cack at the time, and one night this *thing* appeared to me at the foot of me bed, and it frightened the bloody life out of me!' Geezer laughed. 'And I told Ozzy and he wrote the lyrics about it – like warning people against Satanism and stuff.'

Geezer had been living in a one-bedroom flat at the time, which he had painted completely black. 'I had all these inverted crosses all around the place and all these posters of Satan and all that kind of stuff. And I was just lying in bed one night and I woke up suddenly, and there was like this black shape standing at the foot of me bed. And I wasn't on drugs or anything, but for some reason I thought it was the Devil himself...It was almost as if this thing was saying to me, it's time to either pledge allegiance or piss off!' He was so shaken he immediately repainted the flat orange. 'I just went off the whole thing. I took all the posters down, put like proper crucifixes in there, and that's when I started wearing a cross.'

The first time they played the new song live was at a pub called The Poky Hole, in Lichfield, in April 1969. 'In those days when we played everybody would be stood at the bar drinking, not really paying attention,' said Geezer. 'But everybody just stopped dead and...listened. And we finished the song and it just erupted, they went nuts! We couldn't believe it! And we realised then that we were on to something.'

When, not long after, they discovered there was already another band called Earth and decided to change their name, calling themselves after the first song they wrote together was a symbolic choice: the moment when they discovered their true musical identity. Though, of course, Ozzy had his own take on things. 'If anybody said to me, "Ozzy, in the shortest amount of words, how would you describe the music of Black Sabbath?" I would say: "awkward". Just when I'd get a vocal line to go on top of this incredible riff, Tony would fucking change it. Not only the riff but the whole rhythm, and I'd be going, "How am I gonna get *this* to fit *that*?" It was like a challenge. But being so young, there was no musical training, we just sort of did it and that was our sound.

Strange and…awkward. Sometimes, I'd go, "Bill, that don't seem to fit," and he'd go, "Fuck off, Osbourne! You do what you do and I'll do what I do"…'

Recorded in under 12 hours onto two four-track machines in Regent Sound Studios, just off Tottenham Court Road in London, at the tail-end of 1969, the first eponymously titled Black Sabbath album, released in Britain on the Vertigo label in March 1970, was – much to the astonishment of the London-based music critics who had never heard of them – an immediate hit, both at home in Britain, where it reached No. 8, and, even more astonishingly, in America, where it went to No. 23 later the same year and continued hovering ominously in the charts for over 18 months. As Ozzy said, 'Our success wasn't much of a building process, it just happened. All we knew about America was what we'd seen on TV and at the movies. I thought it was all Machine Gun Kelly and *Easy Rider*! When we were told the first album was in the charts there, we thought they were having a laugh. America was where proper groups like The Beatles and the Stones had hits, not the fucking scabby likes of us…'

Ozzy remembers seeing the album at No. 17 in the *Melody Maker* charts and 'my knees went to jelly…I was *speechless*, I couldn't fucking believe it! And from that moment on, my life totally went off like a rocket.' They knew they'd made it, he told me, when they played the Boat Club, in Nottingham, 'and we got £20 instead of our usual fiver. We went there in a car instead of the van, and we found an ounce of hash waiting for us in the dressing room. It was like, "Yes! This is the life!"'

It wasn't until their second album, *Paranoid*, released just six months later, that the instantly identifiable 'Sabbath sound' of legend was first caught masterfully on vinyl. Once again, a straightforward run-through of their ever-evolving live set, most of the material came from their days at the Star Club, in Hamburg, in 1969. The only way they could get through six, 45-minute sets a night, six-nights-a-week, said Ozzy, 'was Tony would solo, we would join in and we would go into this great long jam which songs just sort of came out of. Originally, "War Pigs" was about 40 minutes long.' Thus was born the quintessential 'Sabbath sound': Tony's ability to stack up the riffs and turn them inside out; Geezer's rumbling bass that copied the riff, instead of countering it ('a trick I learned from Jack Bruce'); Bill's jazz-derived percussive flurries; and of course Ozzy's sneering, sing-song vocals. But its most bizarre component derived from the fact that Tony had lost the tips of the two middle fingers on his right hand in a welding accident when he was 17, and now wore tiny home-made plastic 'caps' on his fingers. It gave you an extra chill knowing he couldn't actually 'feel' 50 per cent of what he was playing. 'They said I'd never be able to play again,' Iommi told me, the blow still registering in the lowered tone of his voice. But in truly heroic *Blue Peter* style, he made his own prosthetic fingertips out of an old washing-up liquid bottle. 'I melted it down and made little balls, then got a hot soldering iron and just kept jabbing 'em in. Then I filed them down with sandpaper and glued little strips of leather across the top, so that I could grip the strings, and started to play.'

Tracks like 'Iron Man, 'Fairies Wear Boots', 'Planet Caravan', and of course the 'Paranoid' track itself, ensured that the album would come to be regarded as Sabbath's first real classic – and their first British No. 1. With its white-heat brevity, creepy robotic vocals and one of the greatest rock riffs ever – up there next to 'You Really Got

Me' by the Kinks and '(I Can't Get No) Satisfaction' by the Stones – 'Paranoid' not only gave the band their one and only major hit single in August 1970, it was also destined to became the band's most famous song; their calling card. Instantly becoming the last song of the night at every Ozzy performance (with or without Sabbath) he's ever given since. They made their first appearance on *Top of the Pops* with 'Paranoid' as well, sharing the bill with Englebert Humperdinck, Cliff Richard and Cilla Black. 'Jimmy Savile came up to us and said, "God, your song's pissing up the charts!"' remembered Geezer. 'And I was shocked to hear a DJ swear.'

Still largely innocents abroad, they could not have imagined the chaos that awaited them when they arrived in America for their first tour, in September 1970, where *Paranoid* had reached No. 12 in the album charts. Success, in America, says Ozzy, was 'instant! Instant! I mean, I got scared. They showed us photos of this Black Sabbath parade they'd had in San Francisco, with Anton Levay [self-styled head of the Church of Satan] on top of a fucking Rolls-Royce and I thought, what the fuck? Because at the time you've gotta understand, it was the flower power thing still and it was like this anti-Christ coming into town and they had all these fucking floats and fireworks and people. I remember watching this and going, "That can't be for us, man." I thought it was a joke, you know? It was the Black Sabbath Parade and it was held on his certain fucking astrological day or something. Then when we got there they'd come up to you and go, "Hey, man what star sign are you?" Or, like, "We know that you know that we know, man…" And we'd go, "Yeah, well, good. Keep on knowing, you know?"'

The US dates had already been put back some weeks while the trial of Charles Manson (for the slaying of Roman Polanski's pregnant actress wife, Sharon Tate, and her friends by his psychotic followers) took place, and anything to do with the 'occult' was viewed, briefly, as exceptionally bad taste. And when the band originally wanted to call their second album *War Pigs*, once again their American record company, Warners, forced them to reconsider, afraid that with controversy over the Vietnam War still raging the title would be construed as 'inflammatory' and record stores might refuse to stock it. But that didn't stop millions of disaffected young Americans, living then under the shadow of the draft, picking up on the lines: *'In the fields the bodies burning/as the war machine keeps turning/death and hatred to mankind/poisoning their brainwashed minds...'* and identifying the song 'War Pigs' as an anti-Vietnam statement with real resonance. 'It *was* an anti-Vietnam statement,' insisted Geezer, who wrote the lyrics. 'We used to play American military bases in Germany, and I used to talk to the soldiers and they'd tell me these *horrendous* stories about Vietnam and about all the heroin people used to be on just to get away from it all. And that's where the lyrics came from.'

But it wasn't just protests against the war in Vietnam that their American fans heard in their music. There was also the band's irreligious image to deal with. Or as Tony put it: 'We attracted unbelievable amounts of nutters! There was every kind of Satanist, every Jesus freak.' At one gig, the head of the American Hell's Angels came to give them his blessing. 'About 50 bodyguards came in first,' recalled Geezer. 'Straight into the dressing room, throws all the security out – they're all going "Yes sir, no sir." Then he told us who he was, says "I give you my approval," and that we'd be all right wherever we go – whatever that meant. I mean, it's all like a dream now. They stayed and watched the show and then they went – all in a big motorcycle cavalcade.'

There were so many strange incidents occurring, they began to take them for granted. When they arrived at the Hollywood Bowl, in 1972, and discovered somebody had drawn a large cross in fresh blood across their dressing room door and nailed it shut, they simply kicked it open and ordered a roadie to scrub the door down. Then, on stage that night, Iommi, whose gear was playing up, became so irate that he kicked over a large speaker cabinet, only to reveal a knife-wielding figure dressed in long black robes. 'He was about to stab me,' Iommi shrugged. 'But luckily the roadies tackled him to the floor...I mean, I did feel uncomfortable about it, but I think in them days we were doing so many drugs that it all just flowed into one. "Oh, somebody went to stab me? Oh! Give us another line then!"'

As Iommi suggests, America was also the place where, 'we discovered the old waffle-dust.' Waffle-dust; Charlie; snow. It all meant the same thing: trouble. 'Me and Bill were the worst,' said Ozzy. 'We were both stoned, drunk, fucking pirates going round the place, doing all kinds of fucked-up things...' He shook his head in wonderment. 'I could write a book just on Ozzy Osbourne and Bill Ward episodes that would be fucking outrageous. I mean, he saved me from choking *thousands* of times. I'd do so many reds [Seconals, a powerful tranquilliser] you'd just hear this thump – bang! That would be the sound of your head hitting the table. Me and Bill were the worst. Tony and Geezer would do their own drugs but in their own private space. Me and Bill were like the Drug Commandos – we would never come through the door, it would have to be a plate-glass window or the fucking roof! I mean, we were totally...fucking...out of it! We wouldn't sleep for fucking days. Several times I'd set myself on fire with a fag, lying in bed pissed. And I'd wake up and me chest would be blazing. So as long as we all had a bag of powder and a fucking block of dope and a fucking bottle of booze in the boot and a car to drive and a nice hotel to stay in and do waffle-dust all night, we were happy.'

Soon they had their own coke dealer travelling with them. 'Everywhere we'd go in America this guy would come with us,' said Ozzy, 'For months, years! He'd just turn up. And then one day I was in his room and I opened his bag and there was bags of uncut coke, cut coke, different grade coke. And I picked up one of these bags and there was a revolver underneath and I thought, "This smells like bad news!" But I was coked out me head and you know how paranoid you get as well and I just shit myself!' He added philosophically: 'But, you know, you're never alone with a bag of coke. You could be on a desert fucking island with an ounce of coke and I *guarantee* you about 10 people will knock on your door before the night's out.'

Though such determined drug abuse would, inevitably, result in the long-term destruction of the band, there's no denying that, as Ozzy says, 'We made some of our best albums then.' Indeed, their musical apotheosis – *Master of Reality* (1971), *Volume 4* (1972) and *Sabbath Bloody Sabbath* (1973) – occurred at the very height of their drug-taking. Material for all three albums was written in the same mansion house in Los Angeles that quickly became notorious. 'We used to have coke dealers coming round every day,' remembered Ozzy. 'Only it wasn't just coke by now, it was everything – coke, Demerol [synthetic heroin], acid, dope...' Iommi: 'It became a ritual. Every time we'd do an album we'd get a load of dope and some coke, and whatever else. And of course off we'd go – I never used to want to leave the studio. I'd be in there *all* night *every* night.'

When the comedown finally came in 1974 – the year their management company World Wide Artists went to the wall – it practically finished them off. 'We were four fucking dummies from Birmingham, what did we know?' sighed Ozzy. 'As long as we had a few quid in our pockets and a new car to drive around Birmingham and pull a few tarts, that's all we cared. We never realised the full potential of what we were earning or what the deal was, you know?' The deal was that their management company not only owned all their songs, but all the houses they lived in, the cars they drove, and quite possibly the proverbial shirt off their backs. 'They'd give you money, get you coke, all that kind of stuff,' said Ozzy. 'But they'd always have control over you.'

When did he first suspect that all was not what it should have been at management level? He stared at me woefully. 'It suddenly occurred to me when I went to the office one day and [the managers have] got this whole fucking block of offices and Rolls-Royces for days, and I'm still in a Volkswagen. It doesn't take a cunt to go, "Hang about, that can't be right, can it?"' Sorting through the resultant mess with lawyers, however, 'was like opening Pandora's Box. We couldn't cope. The beauty of the management thing is that once you sign the yin-yang [contract] they can sit on their arse for 10 years and fight legal actions. But you haven't got 10 years to spare. In this business, 10 years is forever, you know? That's always the gun to your head. So you end up settling out of court just to get it out the way – and that's what happened to Sabbath. The music, at the end of the day, was paying for the lawyers' bills and the whole *good idea* that we had originally was so fucking raped by everybody involved it virtually destroyed the band. We kept going for a while longer but it was never the same again. Nobody was ever really happy again…'

Two years of legal wrangles ensued, during which the band fought a losing battle against their still-spiralling drug use and struggled to make another album. '*Sabbath Bloody Sabbath* was our final record, as far as I was concerned,' said Ozzy. 'Then it started to drift around all over the place. Someone would come in with another ounce of fucking powder and you'd be up there talking bullshit again for three weeks.' With the notorious gangster-like figure of Don Arden taking over control of the band's business affairs, the next Sabbath album, the all too aptly titled *Sabotage*, released in July 1975, was, considering the mess their personal affairs were still in, a pretty good piece of work. And despite only getting as far as No. 28 in the US charts, it kept the ailing band's profile high enough to let them carry on headlining their own arena tours.

There were two more Ozzy-era Sabbath albums that performed a similar job, maintaining the band's profile high enough to keep them touring but making no visible impact on the charts – the supremely overindulgent *Technical Ecstasy*, in 1976, and the just plain awful *Never Say Die*, in 1978. But the writing was now on the wall and within weeks of the 1978 world tour ending, Ozzy's departure from the band was announced. 'Eventually we were writing the music for the wrong reasons,' he said, simply. 'We were tired. The drugs and the alcohol were taking their toll…we were all fucked-up and expecting Tony to pull us out of the shit. For which he would spend days in the studio. But we left it upon his shoulders to make us a good record and if it wasn't good and we didn't like it we condemned him for it secretly, in our heads…'

Perhaps their time was simply up; Deep Purple had called it a day the year before; Zeppelin would do the same a year later. With the arrival on the scene of new bands like Van Halen and Judas Priest, it was clear a whole new generation of rockers was now looming on the horizon. Punk had also overtaken Britain – a genre which claimed to despise old-style heavy rockers like Sabbath and Zeppelin. If they had been unfashionable before, now they seemed positively prehistoric. For the first time since they had gatecrashed the party back in 1970, Sabbath had to prove themselves again; and that was a challenge the rest of the band was beginning to believe Ozzy was no longer up to. Even Ozzy says he sensed himself 'losing it. I know it sounds funny but I really did get *paranoid* about stuff like that at the time. I guess we'd been around a while by then but all the faces at the record company seemed to be changing too. It was just a weird time all round. And of course the drugs didn't help. Cocaine had kind of got a-hold of us bad. We were all just totally fucking out of it.'

When Ozzy became so out of control he no longer even bothered turning up for recording sessions – 'I'd completely lost interest by then' – the band bit the bullet and finally fired him. For Ozzy, 'It was like, "Hey, I don't really like what's going on here but what if I jump out of the frying pan into the fire?" And then when I did get fired, I was devastated. Because I thought, right, that's it, it's over, I've lost it all. Bill told me they'd all had a meeting and that I'd gotta go. I was just fucking gutted, you know? I genuinely thought I was on my way to the fucking dole queue.' Even the band was sad to see him go. 'I cried for two days,' Geezer later told me. 'I always said if any of us ever left it wouldn't be Black Sabbath any more – and it wasn't.'

None of which was much help to Ozzy, who was left stranded in LA, renting an apartment at Le Parc hotel in West Hollywood, cutting a swathe through the $90,000 the band had given him to sign away his rights to the name Black Sabbath. 'I remember lying in my pity pot one day at Le Parc,' he later told me, 'doped up to the eyeballs and wondering what the fuck. Suddenly through the open window I could hear some cunt down the street playing a Black Sabbath album. I thought, are you taking the fucking piss, mate?'

No. But someone was…

Act 1
Scene Three:

Don in a Skirt

By the time I got to know her, Sharon Arden was already Sharon Osbourne and the first of her many reinventions had taken place: in this case, from panda-eyed seventies wild child, to ultra-responsible wife, mother and manager of one of the most successful and constantly wayward rock stars of the Eighties. In fact, she was so big and mumsy when I first got to know her it was hard to connect the reality to the image. So incongruous a figure did she cut that it never occurred to me that her giant girth was the result of anything other than the sultan-like opulence she liked to surround herself with. Meanwhile, other musicians would take the piss out of Ozzy behind his back for allowing his 'old lady' to call the shots, not just in terms of his career but his every move. Even then, nearly 25 years ago now, the cry of 'Shaarrroonnn!' was a familiar one to anyone who came into contact with Ozzy for longer than five minutes. Even when she wasn't there he would call out for her sometimes, so used had he become to her doing everything for him, from feeding and clothing him to organising his band, his record contracts and tour commitments, even his short-term memory and quite possibly the tying of his shoelaces.

It wasn't just Ozzy that did what Sharon told him to, either. A formidable figure, few people were ever brave – or stupid – enough to take Sharon on in a head-to-head confrontation. Or at least, none that ever tried it more than once. In that respect, she really did resemble her father – Don Arden, self-styled Al Capone of Rock whose leg-breaking, window-dangling exploits were already legendary in the music business long before Ozzy or Black Sabbath came along to try their luck. Or as Sharon's elder brother David Arden later told me, 'Never forget, that while she's all sweetness and light on the outside, on the inside Sharon is basically Don in a skirt. Fuck around with her and she'll get you. She will.'

The fact is, as Ozzy has always been the first to admit, he was dead lucky that Sharon came along when she did. 'She saved my life, it's as simple as that,' he had told me as far back as 1985. More than 20 years later he was still saying the same thing. 'If I hadn't met her, there's a good chance I would have been dead,' he told me the last time we spoke, during an interview at the Dorchester hotel. 'When I got fired from Sabbath I locked myself away, isolated myself. I checked into a hotel in LA and just ordered booze and pizza over the phone. The coke dealer would come over every day and I would just get loaded. I was there like that for about four months. Never went out, never even opened the drapes. I thought, I'm out of the band, I've got fuck all to live for, my dreams have all been shattered…Then Sharon came along. She showed faith in me from day one. I couldn't believe it, cos I'd given up. But Sharon handled it all. She saved my life.'

Sharon not only pulled him out of the career-grave he had dug himself, she turned him into a bigger star than he or anyone else in

28

Black Sabbath could ever have dreamed possible. And she did it on her own, through sheer force of will. Looking back now, it looks like a great master plan. She certainly made one shrewd move after another when it came to putting Ozzy's name back in lights, but in truth there was a great deal of luck too.

I first got to know Sharon in January 1985, at the two-week-long Rock in Rio festival in Brazil, where Ozzy was appearing alongside a host of other artists, including Rod Stewart, Queen, James Taylor, Iron Maiden, George Benson, AC/DC…loads of others. As chance would have it, Sharon's PA, Lynn Seager, was an old friend who had been shocked to hear how badly my previous meeting with Ozzy had gone; in particular, the last time I'd seen him, a couple of years before, when, now working as a journalist, I had been sent to interview him at the Montcalm hotel in London, only to be greeted by a table full of his drunken cohorts from Birmingham. I didn't even recognise Ozzy as he'd recently shaved all his hair off in an – unsuccessful – attempt to make Sharon abort a tour he was on. Undeterred, Sharon simply had half-a-dozen blond wigs made up for him to wear on stage, which he obediently donned each night for the remainder of the tour, usually pulling it off to uproar from the audience halfway through.

'Awright, mate. What can we do for you?' some fat bloke with short black hair asked me. 'Er, I'm looking for Ozzy,' I said, addressing the table generally. 'Well, you've fucking found him, old bean,' said fat bloke. I looked again and realised my mistake. It was Ozzy. I stammered an apology and sat down. 'Go on then,' one of the others said, 'Ask him something he's never been asked before…'

'Well,' I began, completely thrown. 'What have you been up to lately, Ozzy?'

29

'Fucking hell! Is that the best you can do?' The one who had spoken guffawed, a thick-looking twat with a red beard. Ozzy just sat there staring off into space, a drink in each hand.

I tried again. 'I see you've cut your hair,' I said. 'Why's that then?' Ozzy suddenly sat bolt upright. He leaned forward so that his lips were almost touching the tape recorder and then, very softly, he began making little ooh-oohhh-ooohhhhh sounds, like a chimpanzee. The others started joining in. Soon the whole table was screeching and chattering like monkeys. When it eventually died down, I tried again. But before I could finish speaking the whole table erupted once more in loud animal noises. Ozzy started flapping his arms like a bat. 'I'm just gonna come on stage and bite the heads off the fucking lot of 'em!' he declared. 'And you,' he said, jabbing a finger in my direction, 'You'll be fucking first…'

When I'd told Lynn what a disaster that meeting with Ozzy had been, she suggested I try again. Ozzy wasn't really like that, she insisted. He'd obviously been drunk, having a bad day, surrounded by morons while Sharon was out of sight. 'Come and have lunch,' she said. 'I'll make sure Sharon is there too this time and you'll see a whole new side of Ozzy. And you'll get to meet Sharon. She's a scream. She really is. You'll like her.'

'And there won't be any monkey noises?' I asked, still unsure. 'No monkeys,' she said without smiling, 'I promise.'

We met for lunch the next day by the pool at their hotel on Copacabana beach. It was a beautiful, sunny afternoon, the temperature nudging into the 90s, and I was almost looking forward to it. They were already at the table waiting for me when I got there, Sharon wreathed in welcoming smiles, Ozzy looking down in the dumps. I hadn't realised yet that this was his normal demeanour and that he was actually quite happy and relaxed. Or as happy and relaxed as anyone who had just been released from the Betty Ford Clinic a few weeks before could be. A clean-up cabin for alcoholic film stars and family-rich junkie vagabonds from the West Coast, the Betty Ford boasted a hundred per cent success rate, its clientele in the past including such titanic imbibers as Robert Mitchum, Elizabeth Taylor, and now…Ozzy Osbourne, the 'wild man of rock', as he was known, even back then, in the tabloids.

The question was: would Ozzy *stay* sober? And if so, what would he be like on stage? Had he even done a gig straight before in his life? Or would the self-proclaimed 'born again drunk' crack up under the heat and go mad, demanding a barrel of brandy before he hit the boards? All had seemed well when Ozzy made his first public appearance in Rio that night, sipping lemonade in the bar of the hotel where all the acts were staying, looking trim, tanned, extremely healthy and on his best behaviour. According to rumours though, Ozzy had already broken his vow of abstinence on the flight over, drinking the aircraft dry, finally collapsing in a happy drunken heap in the aisle, where he slept off the remainder of the journey. Though still fragile when I finally sat down with him, his sense of humour had clearly returned and that, it soon became clear, was what was keeping him going through the desert-dry days and achingly sober nights – that and having Sharon constantly by his side.

Sharon was a revelation in the flesh too. I'd heard all the stories of course – how she'd been taught all the dark arts of the music biz while sitting on her evil father's knee; how she didn't suffer fools gladly; how you had to watch your back in case she fired one of her porcupine spines into it when you weren't looking, or, even worse, when you were. In person, however, the first thing that struck me

31

was how pretty she was, how completely different she seemed – much sunnier and outgoing, much more prone to laughter – from the humourless harridan her reputation conjured up. She was also, I couldn't help but notice, quite remarkably fat. Not overweight in that put-on-a-few-pounds way of mums everywhere, but really quite enormous in that way peculiar to Americans of a certain social stereotype. Not that you really noticed until she stood up or you were far enough away. Sitting next to her at the table all I could see were her sparkling eyes and lovely, open face. Very kissable, I thought.

Ozzy ordered the chicken curry. 'And don't forget to leave the head on,' he deadpanned to the waiter but the waiter didn't get it, Ozzy's reputation for biting the heads off winged creatures not having travelled as far afield as Rio – yet. Sharon also ordered the chicken, plus three bottles of iced sparkling mineral water. If Ozzy wasn't able to drink, none of us were.

It was the first time I'd really spoken to Sharon and I discovered that she could be almost as good and as funny a storyteller as her old man. Well, they certainly had a few tales to tell. Before she met Ozzy, Sharon had spent years working for her father, Don. The perfect training, as it turned out, for dealing with her future husband. Having graduated from working as the receptionist in her father's London office, Sharon's first serious job for him had been as 'personal chaperone' to singer Lynsey de Paul, who Don was also then managing. 'We were sharing a hotel room together and by the end of the first tour, I hated her,' Sharon laughed. 'I thought she was a stuck-up little bitch and I'm sure she thought exactly the same of me. Then one night when I was drunk, I'd decided I'd had enough, and I got hold of her suitcase and peed in it...'

These were Sharon's Wild Years. 'I was the original little rich bitch,' she smiled demurely. 'The *mouth* I used to have on me! People used to run when they saw me coming!' 'They still fucking do, some of 'em,' sighed Ozzy. Later on in the seventies, Sharon had also worked with the Electric Light Orchestra (ELO), who Don managed. She frowned and rolled her eyes. 'Oh, God, it was like running an old-age-pensioners' club. They'd all been around for years and all they ever wanted to do on tour was sit in their rooms doing their knitting. We were touring all over the world, going to places most people would only dream of going, and here I was stuck with these dreary old geezers who just weren't *interested*. I thought, I'll go out of my mind if I don't get out of this.'

Ozzy had been Sharon's out. As well as running his own hugely successful record label, Jet, and managing ELO – then one of the most successful groups in the world – Don was also looking after the affairs of Black Sabbath when they decided to get rid of Ozzy, and Sharon had witnessed the fallout firsthand. Chatting about it over lunch that day, according to Sharon, it was all Tony Iommi's idea. 'He did everything he could to get Ozzy out of that band. He'd wait until Ozzy was being driven to distraction by all the wasted time, then when Ozzy hit the bottle and ended up rolling around on the floor he'd call me up and get me to come down to the studio, or wherever. When I got there he'd just point me in the direction of Ozzy, who would either be passed out, or more likely, vomiting all over the floor, and say: "That's what I'm expected to work with! I want him out!" It was a very complicated and extremely touchy time. And mostly for Ozzy, who just didn't know what was going on...'

When Sharon first visited Ozzy at his rented 'pity pot' apartment at Le Parc, 'He was buried in empty pizza boxes, beer bottles and bags of cocaine,' she told me. 'He was in a right state.' Ozzy nodded. 'A typical day for me at Le Parc went like this,' he said. 'Get up, start sniffing cocaine, start drinking lots of beer. I mean, lots of beer. And lots of cocaine, and lots of rude women walking about the place. And I just idled my sweet time away doing what the fuck I wanted. I never used to go out. Never. I spent so much time in this apartment, just sitting around and getting completely out of my head, I knew every inch of all the walls, the ceilings, the floors…It was a bad, bad time for me. I was so fucking lonely. I thought it was the end of me. I couldn't possibly see me carrying on without [Sabbath]. I didn't know the first thing about how to go about it, and I just sat around, getting severely loaded every day and every night. I thought, "Oh well, I'll be out on the street selling hotdogs in two years time", you know?'

Of course, being Ozzy, there were occasionally lighter moments, too. 'I had this gas fire in one of the rooms, and it used to come on automatically – puff! Big jet of flame shoots out the grate. I spent so much time sitting on the couch waiting for this thing to come on, it got to the point where I knew just exactly when it was about to happen, down to the very second. So what I used to do, whenever there was a new chick over, I would start ranting on at her, telling her that all that stuff about black magic and me was *true*, and just as she was on the edge of beginning to believe what I was telling her, I'd suddenly stick my arms out in the air and – puff! Big jet of flame shoots out the wall, and the fire comes on. If they managed to survive that without a heart attack, I'd let 'em hang around for a while…'

He looked across at Sharon. 'Do you wanna tell this next bit?' She shook her head. 'Not while I'm eating,' she joked. 'All right,' he said. 'So…finally, I had no dough. And this guy Mark Nauseef, who was the drummer with Gary Moore [another of Don's artists back then] and who was staying at Le Parc as well, he gave me this envelope full of dough to give to Sharon. He wouldn't be there when she arrived, but I would, and would I do it as a favour? Well, it had about six hundred dollars in it, so I said, "Yeah, sure". This is way before I became involved with Sharon. And I went straight out and bought some cocaine. I got whacked out of my head, and when Sharon comes round the next morning she gives me a severe bollocking. And then she says, "And by the way, we've just fired Black Sabbath, and we want to keep you on". I thought, "Fucking hell, take no notice, this isn't really happening".'

But it was. 'Ozzy had always bugged me,' she said, taking up the story. 'Our paths had crossed, through one thing and another in the business, for years, but I'd only known him well for about three months. That morning I went round to pick up the six hundred dollars Mark had left with Ozzy for me. He'd always, always, bugged me as a person because he was lazy; he was insecure, and dumb! And that bugged me about him, because I knew that he had so much more potential there. And he didn't even know his own strength. He was afraid to use his own strength. He'd always been bullied, all his life he was bullied, and so he had become the way most people would become when they've been bullied non-stop. He was like a squashed man, but I knew that he had just so much more in there, and I was just trying to kick his arse into shape. And when he'd taken that money from me I was furious with him. It was just typical of Ozzy at that time, just typical. And then to do something as stupid as to buy drugs because he thought drugs were gonna help him out of the shit he was in. Stuck in a hotel room in Los Angeles, with no band, and he wants to sit there taking drugs. He was just not helping himself.'

Ozzy was still contractually tied to Don but with Arden then more preoccupied with the burgeoning success of ELO – his cut from their vast record sales allowing him to purchase Howard Hughes' famous old Hollywood mansion around this time for $2 million cash – the 'old man', as both Ozzy and Sharon still referred to him, was happy to let his daughter take up the slack and begin overseeing the day-to-day running of Ozzy's post-Sabbath career. He had originally considered designating the task to his son David. But David's baby daughter Charlotte had just been born prematurely and he was understandably more focused on his young family. So the job went to Sharon, who was delighted. 'I think she felt sorry for me,' said Ozzy. 'Everybody up to that point was going, "You dummy, you idiot, you can't do fuck all". All my life I used to be called a dummy. She was the first one who didn't.'

Though it didn't become apparent to me until many years later, there was also another, further motivation behind Sharon's desire to take up the cudgels on Ozzy's behalf. She had earlier been in a tempestuous affair with Tony Iommi, who was married at the time, and he ended it with Sharon when it became clear she was becoming emotionally involved. The break-up had been messy and acrimonious. According to Don, 'There was a big row and she ended up smashing him over the head with a frying pan.'

Of course, as Don also used to say, 'You can't polish a turd.' A saying that has since become a music business maxim for the need to have the talent in place first before you can build a career around it. And while industry observers considered Ozzy a washed-up has-been, Sharon was one of the few people shrewd enough to realise he still had a chance of making a success of his career. 'Ozzy had always been the focal point of Black Sabbath anyway,' she said, 'and it was always Ozzy the kids wanted to see the most, and though a lot of record companies didn't agree, I knew the size of the following that Ozzy still had. As far as I could see, there was definitely a career there for Ozzy, it was just a question of getting him to deal with himself and control himself.'

But getting Ozzy Osbourne to 'deal with himself' and – good luck – 'control himself' was something else entirely. Not having managed to achieve either of those goals himself in his 11 years with Sabbath, how was Sharon going to manage that trick now? The answer, she decided, was to take complete control. The first order of the day: to try and restore his self-esteem. So before she even began thinking about helping him form a new band, she took Ozzy out of Le Parc and installed him in one of the cottages on Don's vast estate in Beverly Hills, then bought Ozzy some clothes to wear, sprucing up his previously dour, soiled T-shirt and week-old-jeans appearance with some high-priced items hand-picked to make Ozzy look every bit the star, both on and offstage. 'I thought, no one is going to take him seriously if he doesn't take himself seriously,' she reasoned. 'They were all expecting this drunken slob to walk through the door. I wanted him to make a different sort of impression. So I got him some expensive clothes, and some jewellery to wear. Made him shave and have some highlights put in his hair. He ended up looking like a million dollars and feeling like it, too.'

'I don't know about a million dollars,' Ozzy interjected, his mouth full of chicken head curry, 'more like fifty quid.'

'Pay no attention to him,' she said. 'He wouldn't know anyway, he's never paid a bill in his life…'

While all this undoubtedly had its effect, ironically what actually propelled Ozzy back into the limelight was a trick not even Sharon or her father could have dreamt up – and it certainly had nothing to do with making over his image. It was, if anything, one of the most ill-mannered, drunken, couldn't-give-a-fuck actions of his entire life: biting the head off a live dove at a CBS Records convention in 1981.

Having steered Ozzy through his first post-Sabbath solo album, *Blizzard of Ozz* – a Top 10 hit in Britain in 1980 – Sharon was frustrated at the lack of support for the album in America. Not least, as Ozzy was signed to her father's label, Jet – distributed by CBS. 'After years of working in this business, you get to know straight off when a record company is behind your product,' said Sharon, 'and basically, Jet and CBS in America didn't seem to give a damn about Ozzy, at that time. The guys that worked out on the street, the ones that had the closest contact with us, they were into it, but the ones that sat back in their offices and signed the cheques didn't seem to be interested. So we thought, "Well, what are we gonna do". Ozzy had been invited along to this CBS Records convention, along with a lot of other acts connected to the company, and it was just one of those hello, hello, stab you in the back as soon as you walk out of the doors, parties, all that crap – getting introduced to people who forget your face five minutes later. That's when we came up with the idea of the doves…'

Well, sort of. The original idea, in fact, had been much tamer. Due to give a short speech to the assembled CBS executives, Sharon had thought it would be a nice idea for Ozzy to release three white doves into the air at the end of it. 'Don't ask me fucking why, but that was the deal,' said Ozzy. 'Trouble was I'd already drunk a bottle of brandy that morning and by the time I got there I was fucked. I just remember this PR woman going on and on at me. In the end, I said, "Do you like animals?" Then pulled out one of these doves and bit its fucking head off. Just to shut her up – spitting the head out on the table – and she fell to the floor screaming. That's when they threw me out. They said I'd never work for CBS again but Sharon started working the phones and that night it was on the TV news. That's when the first album started shifting…'

'He had these fucking doves in his coat pocket when we arrived there, and when he took one of them out and bit its bloody head off, I ran away!' laughed Sharon. 'He let two of them fly off and all these silly girls were sitting there smiling and sighing quietly, and then Ozzy grabs the last dove and yanked its head off. I couldn't believe my eyes!'

Escorted from the building by CBS security guards, the story made the *Six O' Clock News* that night on TV. By the following morning it was in newspapers all over the world. Before you could say Public Enemy Number One, Ozzy Osbourne had suddenly become the most talked about rock celebrity in the world. Suddenly, everybody had an opinion on this Osbourne character. Some wanted to string him up, in particular the Humane Society of America, who started a campaign to ban his concerts in America. Even some of the old Sabbath fans were shocked, the letters' pages of music magazines across the globe suddenly filled with debates about what had happened. Had it been an accident? (Not really.) Had Ozzy simply lost his mind? (In a way, yes.) Was it all just some stupid publicity stunt? Definitely, except not so stupid once you started adding up the rapidly increased record sales.

Yet no one was more outraged than Ozzy's own record company, who now banned him from even entering the CBS Records building in Los Angeles, even threatening him with being thrown off the label. 'One of the lawyers from CBS said to me over the phone that if I wanted to see Ozzy buried, just carry on doing what we were doing,' recalled Sharon. 'Meaning, they were ready to kill the album stone dead in America. They just could not handle what Ozzy had done. And it was all so perfect really. This was right before [Ozzy's] first US tour and, believe me, it really worked for us. Everywhere Ozzy went, he was selling out, and tripling his album sales everywhere he played.'

To rub it in, Ozzy's US stage show now featured a catapult that hurled meat into the audience. 'We had a leaflet mailed out to all the towns he was appearing in and it read something like, "Bring your liver to an Ozzy show – and he'll throw it back at you". The response we got was amazing, I'd never seen anything like it!' Ozzy shook his head and grinned. They'd fire offal into the audience from the catapult, 'And we'd get the contents of about 17 million butchers' shops chucked back at us! You should have seen the stuff we used to get – snakes, rats, dead cats, lizards, the whole fucking business. One night we had a swamp frog thrown at us, which is a huge great thing. The fucking thing landed on its back right in front of me, and I looked down and at first I thought it was a baby child. That's when I thought the whole thing was getting a bit over the top. One night they turned a guy away at the door because he was carrying an ox's head under his arm!'

When one night a bat arrived at his feet, Ozzy grabbed it and thrust its head into his mouth, assuming it was a plastic toy. When the poor creature started to flap around and wriggle in his mouth, Ozzy freaked for a moment, and in the panic to get the bat out, off came its head – scrunch! 'I used to joke and say it tasted like a Ronald McDonald's,' he said, 'but the truth is I thought it was a fucking toy. Someone threw it on stage at a gig in America and it must have been stunned by the lights or something cos it was dead still when I picked it up. I put it in my mouth as a joke. Then its fucking wings started flapping and I ripped it out of my mouth but its head came off! The worst part was the anti-rabies injections I had to have in the arse the next day. Really fucking painful…'

Again, though, it all just added to the publicity Ozzy was now receiving everywhere he went. By the end of 1981, *Blizzard of Ozz* had notched up nearly five million sales in America alone. Not only had Ozzy somehow achieved the previously thought impossible and actually survived his ousting from Black Sabbath, he had gone one better by turning himself into an even bigger star without them. He and Sharon had much to feel proud of as they busied themselves getting ready for the release of Ozzy's follow-up solo album, *Diary of a Madman*. By then, however, an even more significant event had occurred in both their lives, something so unexpected neither of them could quite believe it at first – nor anybody else that knew them. Ozzy and Sharon had fallen in love.

Married at the time of his sacking from Sabbath, Ozzy's original plan had been to take his severance payment and return to England to his wife Thelma and their two children, Jessica (born in 1971) and Louis (born 1975). They would open and run a wine bar together. When Ozzy had outlined his plan to Sharon, however, she had burst out laughing. She laughed about it again now over lunch in Rio. 'Could you imagine?' he chortled. 'Ozzy running a wine bar? Talk about putting the lunatic in charge of the asylum!'

During their months working so closely together though, Ozzy had come to rely on Sharon so totally he began to forget not just about his plan to retire to England and his fantasy wine bar, he seemed to forget he was married too. Living with the Arden family at their palatial Hollywood mansion, he began to fall for Sharon in a big way. 'She was always a very classy woman, smart and outgoing. I came from a totally different background, not as wealthy or educated, and I thought she was an impressive woman. I was attracted to her, but at that time I was married. My marriage wasn't going well, but I wasn't looking for a wife. Then one thing led to another, and I fell in love with her.'

What was it that attracted him to her, though, I asked? 'Her laugh,' he said simply. 'When she laughs it makes the whole world worth living in. And we just get on together. For a long time, people would think we were brother and sister, that we even looked alike. Then one time, she was taking Gary Moore and his girlfriend to San Francisco for the weekend and she says to me, "Do you wanna come, too?" I thought, "Fucking hell, it's on!" But then I got so fucked-up I couldn't find her room. So the magical deed didn't happen for a long while.' Even then, 'I was drunk and, like a fucking idiot, I kept calling Sharon by my first wife's name.'

It happened, in fact, one night during rehearsals for his first UK tour in November 1980, back in the bar at their hotel, when a drunken, doe-eyed Ozzy suggested they finish off the evening in his room. It was hardly the first time he had propositioned Sharon but this was the first time she ever said yes. 'I got her drunk and leapt on her,' he joked. But for Sharon it meant much more than that. 'When I met Ozzy, who was so truthful and just an honest person, I fell for him hook, line and sinker. Yes, he was a rock'n'roller who did crazy things, but crazy was nothing to what was going on in my house.' Plus, they made each other laugh. As she said years later, 'He loved me the way I was. I'd never want to make love with the light on. I would roll myself not only in the sheet, but the duvet and the bloody pillows. But Ozzy would laugh. He'd tell me I was daft.'

Now, four years on, not only was Ozzy a bigger star than he'd ever been in Sabbath, he was also the father of two beautiful infant daughters, Aimee and Kelly – and though they didn't know it yet, a third child on the way later that year. Biggest surprise of all, he was also, post-Betty Ford at least, surprisingly clean and sober. For now, anyway. A transformation he was the first to admit was down entirely to his relationship with Sharon.

Things had gotten off to a rocky start though – and not just musically. 'Some of the worst, most violent fights I've ever had have been with her,' said Ozzy, jerking his thumb. 'Far worse than any bloke you might have a punch-up with. She's fuckin' vicious, she is.' Sharon nodded. 'When we first met,' she confessed, 'we were both drinking and it was just insane. Being with Ozzy meant waking up with a raging hangover every day.' Indeed, stories of the early days of their relationship – both personal and professional – were legion. How she had tried to win his respect in the early days by showing him she could actually match him drink for drink if she wanted. Not only that, but she could match him for loud obnoxious behaviour too, if that was what he wanted, standing in the bar with him mouthing off to anybody who came near her, even throwing a punch or two when the occasion demanded it. So much so that by the time Ozzy was out on tour again and the pair had not-so-secretly become lovers their joint reputation for drunken outbursts now preceded them, wrecking hotel rooms, hurling furniture, telling each other to fuck off and – almost certainly – 'calling a cunt a cunt' as Ozzy put it, at the tops of their voices. On one memorable occasion Sharon was so pissed off with Ozzy she threw an expensive bottle of perfume straight at him. Too drunk and stoned to move out of the way in time, the bottle smashed against his head and shattered into a million pieces. A doctor had to be called out in the middle of the night to treat him for cuts and contusions.

'Our fights were legendary,' said Sharon. 'We'd beat the shit out of each other. At a gig Ozzy would run off stage during a guitar solo to fight with me, then run back on to finish the song. We'd both drink until we blacked out and wake up the next morning with black eyes and bruises – he'd hit me, I'd hit him.' She shook her head. 'Then one morning, I realised. I thought, we're never gonna get anywhere like this. At least one of us has to be straight, and I knew it wasn't going to be *him*. So I stopped there and then. That was it.'

'It was unbelievable,' said Ozzy. 'I couldn't do it, personally. Just stop cold like that. But Sharon did and thank fuck she did cos if it had been down to me we'd both be out selling hotdogs by now.' They sat there grinning at each other. Sharon reached over and squeezed his hand. I sat there staring at them, not knowing what to make of it all. They looked like the happiest couple in the world. Yet they had been through so much. It was a wonder they had been able to stick with each other through so much...shit. There was no other word. 'She's not only a great wife and manager,' he said, 'she's also a great mate. Of course, I have to say that cos she's sitting here...'

And it was Sharon who had more or less dragged Ozzy to the Betty Ford Clinic. What was that like, I wondered? 'Oh, you know,' Ozzy shrugged. 'They talk to you and try and get you to see that what you're doing is fucking things up for you...I remember them showing us films of people spending their lives doing all the bad things, like drinking too much and snorting too much coke. They would be like these little soap operas where you see this guy and his wife going to a party, then the guy gets totally fucked up out of his head on booze and things start falling apart in his life. But that bastard tickled me! He was having such a good time at this party, I started cheering and clapping every time he chucked one

44

back or snuck off for a sneaky line. That's when they decided to ban me from attending the film classes. I was enjoying them too much!'

He looked at Sharon somewhat guiltily but if she was concerned you'd never had guessed it from the inscrutable smile on her face. 'Ultimately,' he said, 'you've got to want to stop fucking up your life. *You've* got to want it. They can give you all the pills and potions in the world, which is what I had at first, but if you don't want it to work then you needn't worry, it won't. And if you're taking a pill as a substitute for a drink, you're still as fucked up as you were on the drink, except now it's a pill. I'd rather have a drink myself...'

He paused. 'What's that smell?' he asked, wrinkling his nose theatrically.

'I don't know,' said Sharon, 'but I'm eating it.'

'Oh God, you're not eating it if it stinks like that, are you? It smells like someone's crapped their pants...'

'It might be the olives,' I said.

'It could be the cheese,' said Sharon.

'Smegma!' cried Ozzy. 'It smells like somebody's guts got hit!'

Sharon leant over to sniff the cheese. 'I think it smells quite pleasant actually,' she smiled.

'Well, you can rub it round your arsehole then, can't you?' he said, braying Eeyore-ishly and the pair of them dissolved into fits of laughter again.

Just then, music started blaring out from somewhere up above us, so loud we could no longer hear ourselves speak. I recognised it: 'Green Onions' by Booker T & The MGs. We all looked up to a balcony overlooking the pool.

'That'll be fuckin' Rod Stewart again!' Ozzy hollered above the din.

'That cunt's being playing that same fucking record for two days now. I'm gonna swing for him when I see him!'

'He's just fucking jealous cos Ozzy's bigger than him these days,' Sharon yelled in my ear.

Sharon sent a minion off to see what he could do about getting Stewart to stop but it soon became obvious there would be no point continuing. Not today, anyway. As we strolled back to the reception area, away from the noise, I asked a couple of last-minute questions. Ozzy was now in his late-thirties, old for a heavy metal star (or so it seemed back then). When did he think he'd have had enough of this?

'What, retire, you mean? Put it this way, I've got a house in London but I'm never there. So that's my dream for the future: to eventually get home, close the door, put the stereo on, and that's it. Play pool in my pool-room and sit in my bar with no drinks. Sharon keeps saying to me, "Do you want to be singing when you're 40?" But I don't know. I keep saying to myself, "I'll give it another two years, I'll give it another three years". But until there comes a day when the band stop giving people fun, until the kids stop having fun, until *I* stop having fun, I'll probably keep going. It's too fucking late to stop now anyway, ain't it? And I've got a lot of respect for the kids. They get on your fuckin' nerves sometimes, but if it wasn't for them there wouldn't be a Rod Stewart, there wouldn't be an Ozzy Osbourne, there wouldn't be a Queen, there wouldn't be *any* of us poncing around like pricks. As long as my band don't look like a darts team on stage, that's all I worry about, do you know what I mean? It's the easiest thing in the world to be a cunt all your life. It's somebody else's turn now to be a cunt. I don't wanna be a fucking douche-bag that goes up there every night, a fat, boring old fart...'

A few nights later we bumped into each other again, this time at a restaurant called Muiro's, reputedly one of the finest meat-eateries in Rio. While the waiters threw huge skewers of barbecued flesh onto our yawning plates, Ozzy reminisced about his time in Black Sabbath. 'It was such a laugh in the early days,' he recalled. 'We treated nothing seriously. Let's face it, we couldn't treat anything seriously outside of playing, we were all too bloody thick. I remember Tony and Bill doing this live radio show once, and the interviewer asked Tony who the biggest influence was on his guitar playing and he just sat there and went: "Er…um…ah…er…well…er…let's see…er…Bert". The DJ was like, "Bert? Bert who?" Stupid sod was talking about Bert Weedon. Then Bill, who's been sat there saying nothing for the last half an hour, suddenly leans over and asks the interviewer if he minds if he just clears his throat. The bloke says, "No, of course no", so Bill leans into the microphone and goes: "Bollocks! Fuck! Cunt! Piss! Shit! Bollocks! Fuck! Bastard!" Interview over…'

He went on to another pet hate: rock stars that pretend to dislike being recognised but secretly love it. 'You see these fuckers hanging out in nightclubs in New York or somewhere, and they're all walking around wearing bloody sunglasses. They can't see a fucking thing and spend two hours talking to a bloody brick wall, acting cool. Actually, that reminds me of the time I was just leaving this club pissed out of me brains. As I got to the door Roger Taylor from Queen was standing there with his shades on, and he stops me and says hello. I looked at him and said, "Who the hell are you?" And he shoves his bloody sunglasses down his nose, peers over the top of them and says, "It's me, man, Roger". And of course I knew who he was, I was just pissed out of me head. So I looked at him and goes, "Bollocks! Queen just ripped off everything they ever did from Sabbath!" And I walked out the door. Can you imagine his face?' He roars with laughter. 'You should have seen him trying to figure that one out! Queen ripped off Sabbath! He hasn't spoken a word to me from that day to this...'

I shook his hand and we said goodbye, then kissed Sharon on the cheek. As they made their way together down the steps towards the waiting limo, I could hear his voice still going, 'Shaarrooonnn...'

Act 1
Scene Four:

A Child of the Grave

As the years passed and I got to know both Ozzy and Sharon better, I realised two things. Firstly, that the double-act they had developed together was more than just a handy way of deflecting awkward questions. It was actually based on who they really were. And, secondly, that one thing they really had in common was that in their own different ways they had both suffered from grossly dysfunctional childhoods: Ozzy as the product of a drunken working class background where violence and swearing weren't second nature, they were first; Sharon as the attention-seeking product of a bizarrely constructed home life where the house was always full of famous artists and cauliflower-eared thugs but very little love and affection. That it was their peculiar backgrounds – so different on the surface, so alike underneath in their neediness and desperate search for love, real love – that drew them to each other and kept them glued together, through the tantrums and the tears, the rewards and the setbacks, like Siamese twins.

Hardly a natural singer but a born frontman, as Ozzy told me, the seeds of his later stardom 'all goes back to when I was a kid at school. Really, I was a quiet kid, but if I was surrounded by people, I thought I had to be eccentric for them to like me. I always worked along the lines of: if you can't beat 'em, make 'em laugh. Do anything you can to keep them on your side. And if they still don't like you after that, burn their fucking house down,' he cackled.

It was a formula that would see him through a childhood characterised by hardship and degradation. The fourth child of six, his father John Thomas was a toolmaker and his mother, Lillian, worked at the local Lucas car plant. All eight of them lived at 14 Lodge Road, a small terraced house in Aston, a place Ozzy and I would visit together many years later, now owned by an Asian family, who allowed us inside to look around. 'We were rammed in here,' said Ozzy. 'It was nuts. And there was never enough money. It used to tear me apart to see my mother crying cos she hadn't got enough dough to spend on bills and things.' It was because of distressing scenes like this that Ozzy took to breaking into gas meters and stealing the money. 'Every few weeks a guy from the gas company would come by to empty the meters of all the money. Only by then I'd usually been in there and got hold of it first.'

As a young boy, Ozzy – as he'd been quickly nicknamed in the school playground – had such a vivid imagination he would find himself prone to strange obsessions, like the phase he went through when he believed his father would die while he was sleeping. A night worker at the local GEC factory, Ozzy would creep up the stairs to his bedroom where he was sleeping during the day 'and prod him to make him move or grunt or something, anything to prove he wasn't dead. I used to be really convinced he'd die if I didn't do something. Looking back, I think what I really wanted was to actually see him dead. I was very afraid of all sorts of things when I was a child.' He added: 'My home life when I was growing up as a child was like a battlefield a lot of the time. My parents gave all they could, but it was never enough for me. I wanted everything I could lay my hands on. I wanted to be Superman. I wanted to be the Devil! And I always had a big thing about the darker side of life, the morbid grey side of things.'

Apart from mother Lillian – 'She was the one that used to drive me a lot because I never saw much of my dad due to his working nights' – he was close to his older sister, Jean. 'She was fucking great. Even now she helps me out and she gets me through the day.' Whenever it 'all got on top' in his Sabbath days he would 'turn up on her doorstep drunk as a fool. She's a good girl, Jean. I never got to know the other guys half as well. There was Iris and Gillian, and then me and my two brothers Paul and Tony. What used to keep us all together, and one of the things I like to remember from those days, are the family get-togethers we used to have, big sing-songs in the house. It was great when my old man came home with a few beers inside him, he'd start reeling off a few renditions of old-time pub songs like "Show Me the Way to Go Home". I can still remember sitting outside the local boozer when I was just a young kid waiting for my dad to come out on a Sunday afternoon. By about half past one you'd hear all the blokes inside singing. And it really sounded great! I got all my early musical influences from pub sing-songs.'

Never remotely academically motivated, Ozzy recalls spending his early years at Prince Albert Road Juniors primary school trying to fit in. Regular time-honoured playground games, like football, bored Ozzy. 'I pretended to be into it for a while, but I could never stand it. A bunch of fools running around a field kissing each other…'

Instead, Ozzy fell into the dubious pastime of organising playground hanging squads. 'We used to get a bit of rope or a clothes line, then find a suitable victim and hang him from the roof of the toilets. We never actually killed anyone though,' he adds, sounding disappointed. 'Basically, I was a very private child. I'm a very private person now, but I was eccentric as a child in the respect that although I want to remain private, when I'm cornered, when I'm surrounded by lots of other people, I feel I have to be an eccentric for them to like me. I always wanted people in those situations to accept me and like me, and I'd really go out of my way to get them to. That's the way I've been. I wasn't a particularly hard kid, but I got round all that by befriending the school bully, who was a real hard case. I figured if I could make the school bully laugh he'd be my mate and no one would ever hit me because they'd know he was there to hit them back for me.'

By the time Ozzy moved in his adolescence to Birchfield Road Secondary Modern in nearby Perry Barr, he was a Teddy Boy. 'Teddy Boys always fascinated me. I loved hanging around the cafes and coffee houses, playing pinball. I was into a typical backstreet upbringing, nipping round the back of the coalhouse with a packet of five cheap cigarettes and a penny book of matches. I got more fun throwing bricks in the canal than I ever did at any school. I lived in a tiny place with no money and nothing to do and school just bored me to tears. I never even saw the sea until I was 14; just once, in Sunderland where my family had relatives.'

By now Ozzy was listening to his first rock'n'roll records. 'School felt like such an unnatural thing for me to be doing, and the music always felt good. But it always got me into trouble at school because of it. I'd get sent home for wearing winkle-pickers and blue jeans instead of their boring grey flannels.' Up until then, music and singing was something 'I never even really thought about.' When a boy from the year above him at school, named Tony Iommi, started bringing his Fender guitar to school, Ozzy duly noted 'all the girls fawning over him. I remember thinking, what a great way to pull birds.' But any further thoughts of music-making were rarely explored.

'When I was younger I never really got into bands or singers much. There were records I liked, but I didn't care who made them. My sister Jean used to bring home Chuck Berry records and stuff which was all right, but I was never a big fan of anybody in particular. Not until the birth of The Beatles, which was probably the biggest turn-on of my life up to then.' It wasn't just the music that appealed, though. 'It was as much the fact that they were four guys like me who'd come from the back streets of Liverpool, opened all the doors, and proved it could be done.'

At 14 he had formed his own imaginary version of The Beatles, which he called the Black Panthers, spray-painting the name on walls of buildings all over Aston. 'When I go back to Aston now I can still find walls with "Black Panthers" spray-painted on them. And other bits of graffiti I did are still there. Strange things too like, OZZY – IRON MAN [a later Black Sabbath song] and IRON MAIDEN. This was like years before Sabbath or Iron Maiden existed. Maybe the instinct for it was always there, I dunno, and maybe I just didn't know what to channel it into…'

Instead, weekends would see him and his mates acting as 'car minders' at local soccer matches. 'The Aston Villa supporters would drive up on a Saturday morning and park their cars all around the outside of the football field. [We] used to hang around waiting for the bloke to get out of his car, and then we'd all rush up and say, "Mind your car for you, mister?" And of course it was pure blackmail really.

The guy wouldn't dare say no in case you vandalised his car while he was off watching the match. We ended up making a fortune at that racket.' As usual, he went too far though. When one day he got the bright idea of insisting one of his 'clients' needed their car washed as well as minded, he set to work on the paintwork with a scouring pad. When the enraged owner returned to find the paintwork on his car destroyed, he forwarded the bill to Ozzy's furious father. 'He nearly killed me when he got stuck with that bill.'

In the desperate never-ending hunt for money, there was also a succession of part-time jobs while he was still at school, including a newspaper round, a grocery delivery round, and another job delivering big sacks of King Coal at a 'tanner-a-time' (two-and-half-pence in today's money). It was the same story when Ozzy finally left school in 1963, plunging into one boring poorly-paid job after another, from labouring on a building site ('Now *that's* what you call work!') to testing car horns at the same Lucas plant as his mum ('Definitely the stupidest job I ever had') to working as a plumber's mate, which he had 'always fancied for some reason' but which he hated because the busiest times were always in winter, when frozen pipes burst. 'You'd sit all day in somebody's loft or squatting under the kitchen sink and you'd have to keep biting your fingertips to get the blood circulating. If you could find a hot pipe anywhere on the job it was like heaven. The plumber needed a crowbar to get my hands off it.'

The 'best job I ever had,' he told me, had been at a slaughterhouse in Digbeth. 'The first day I was there almost did me in. They gave me the shittiest job they could find: cutting open sheep stomachs and taking out all the revolting shit that was inside them. It was so vile I was throwing up all day. After a while, though, I really got into it.

I loved killing animals! I used to stick them, stab them, chop them, totally torture the fuckers to death,' he guffawed.

'Jesus,' I said, shifting uncomfortably in my seat. 'You're making me sick.'

He shrugged. 'I used to take a lot of speed at the time and I would be out of my fucking head all day. I used to kill a minimum of two hundred and fifty cattle a day and then get onto the pigs and sheep…'

'Christ, stop!' I pleaded.

'If the pigs had worms I used to bite their heads off. Even back then the people I worked with thought I was mad. But, you know, live and let die…'

But even a speed-crazed teenage hoodlum like Ozzy couldn't stand working in a place like that for long. 'It was the smell that got to me in the end. No one would ever sit next to me on the bus home at night, I felt like a leper. Even the bus conductor stuck his head out the window when he took my fare! That and the rats! The rats at the slaughterhouse were all absolutely fucking gigantic, and they were everywhere you went! I'm still shit scared of rats today; they're my worse phobia.' Soon he was back on the dole, scrounging around for another dead-end job. Or pretending to. 'I'd already decided I didn't want to spend the rest of my life working in a factory.' He knew 'it would take something extra-special to get you out of a dump like that, but I hadn't thought of doing music yet.'

By now he was a Mod: dressing in mohair suits and getting high on amphetamines. 'People never believe me when I tell them,' Ozzy smiled. 'But I used to have cropped skinhead hair and a mohair suit. You had to look like that to get into the All Nighters.' The All Nighters were 24-hour dance clubs that stayed open all weekend. 'I used to go there to score speed. I tried it all: black bombers, dexies, double dex, triple dex, whites, blues, anything I could lay my hands on just to get that buzz going. I'd be up all night and come home the next morning with my eyeballs hanging out, and I'd go into the local cafe for a few mugs of tea. When it was late enough I'd have to go home and pretend that I was dog tired. I'd go off to bed and lie there awake all day with my heart pounding like a drum, counting the bricks and the cracks in the ceiling. And then I'd have to go down to Sunday dinner and make out I was really hungry. It was disgusting.'

He went on: 'We used to fight other kids a lot. The newspapers always called it a Mods versus Rockers conflict, but the kind of Mods I hung around with were just into fighting. We used to get the old dustbin lids out and carry fucking iron pokers into fights with us.' Vicious pitched battles would take place all over Birmingham. On one particularly over-the-top occasion, Ozzy found himself deliberately trying to drown someone. 'I could be a vicious little fucker. And I remember there was one time when some other kid hit me smack on the head with a brick. I got up off the ground with my head all swollen and bleeding and said, "Missed!".'

Meanwhile, Ozzy had a new job, working at the same Lucas plant as his mum, sitting in a soundproofed room all day testing new car horns. Ozzy later jokingly described it as, 'My first real musical training. It probably explains the sort of music I got into later.' In fact, he couldn't stand it and soon left. 'I remember this old boy in there at the plant called Harry. He'd worked at Lucas for over 30 years. Leaning over the conveyor belt every day had made him look like a paralysed monkey.' All that was keeping Harry going was the thought of his gold watch when he retired. 'I thought to myself, "Fucking hell, if I wanted a gold watch that bad I'd go smash a jeweller's window".'

Now 17 and still going nowhere, in fact petty crime was exactly what he turned to, beginning with the planned break-in of the clothes shop his sister, Jean, worked for. 'It was at the back of our house – Sarah Clarke's I think it was called – and my idea was to break in and steal a load of jumpers and sweaters, and sell them later.' However, it was 'pitch black in there' and it hadn't occurred to the apprentice thief to bring a torch with him. 'Eventually I got away with an armful of gear, but when I got it outside it turned out to be stacks of kids' clothes and women's tights. There I was, Super Hood, loaded to the gills with stockings and kids' jumpers!'

So he tried again, elsewhere, but was never very good at it. 'I really panicked,' he said. 'The fear of being caught when you're doing a job paralyses your brain.' He was 'such a fucking dumbo,' he said, 'I used to wear these gloves with the thumb missing on one of them, so I always left a perfect thumbprint on every shop I ever broke into. The local cops must have been led by Inspector Clouseau not to catch on.'

For a while, he teamed up with another local youth, whose father was a drunken wastrel who kicked him out every morning. With nothing else to do, Ozzy's new pal would roam the streets keeping a lookout for likely targets for the rogue attentions of himself and Ozzy. It was one such morning that he hit upon a house in the richer part of town where for several mornings he had observed the same man leave the building at exactly the same time, 7.00am. Perfect, they decided, and plans were made to rob the joint. What neither would-be cat burglar knew until it was too late was that the other occupant of the house was a night-worker who went to bed at six every morning. 'I was keeping watch downstairs while [my mate] shinned up a drainpipe,' said Ozzy. 'The next thing I know [he's] flying straight out of the bedroom window off the big end of this bloke's number nine sized boot. [He] landed in the street and broke his leg. Then the guy came outside of the house and beat the hell out of him. After that the guy called the police and [my mate] was well and truly nicked. You'd have thought that would be enough to put me right off any more criminal dealings. But it didn't.'

The archetypal villain returning to the scene of the crime, Ozzy, now solo, again broke into the Sarah Clarke clothes shop, only this time he was caught and arrested, according to the official charge sheet, for 'Breaking and Entering and Stealing Goods to the value of twenty-five pounds'. Tried, found guilty and fined £40 – an astronomical sum for the Osbourne family in those woebegone days – when he was unable to come up with the money he was sentenced instead to three months in prison. Ozzy's father, John Thomas, might have helped pay the fine, but decided that going to prison would knock some sense into his wayward son's head. Despite going down on bended knees to beg, John let Ozzy be interned at Winson Green Prison – the cheerless final home of infamous serial killer Fred West, who committed suicide in his cell there in 1995 – where he eventually served six weeks of his three-month sentence. Over the next 20 years Ozzy Osbourne would reside in locked cells of all shapes and sizes around the world for all manner of strange and heinous crimes (mainly unloading his bladder in places and on things a man shouldn't, and mainly in America), but this was his first serious bust, and the first time in prison for a very young man.

'I was terrified,' he told me. Not just because of the constant threat of violence from the other, older prisoners but because of the fear of being raped. 'In prison you're not talking about normal gay guys,' he pointed out, 'You're talking about murderers, or GBH (grievous bodily harm) merchants who go gay temporarily because there ain't no skirt around in prison. The nearest thing they can find to a woman is a teenage boy. So there I am in prison with these people and I've got long hair, and wallop! They're around me like bees round a honey pot. I was shit scared. One big murderer tried to fuck me up the arse one day, so I crowned him with a fucking metal pisspot and ended up in solitary confinement for three days. But I found my best defence was my old school standby: make 'em laugh. I got through a few hard times, and a lot of tough situations, by making people laugh and humouring them. I know six weeks doesn't sound a lot, but it seemed like six years when I was in there, especially when I spent time in solitary…To this day I can't stand being on my own for any length of time.'

It was also at Winson Green that Ozzy got his first tattoos. Self-administered, using the age-old prison technique of pin and graphite, he scratched O-Z-Z-Y across the knuckles of his left hand. He also tattooed two smiling faces on his bare knees to cheer him up, he said, when he woke up every morning. Nevertheless, the weeks dragged by. After a while it wasn't just the gory tales the mass murderer with whom he shared a cell regaled him with that kept Ozzy awake at night. It was the thought of the old workmate from the slaughter-house who had been jailed for stealing 400 cigarettes and four boxes of Mars Bars; the self-styled 'hard man' who used to cry himself to sleep at night while Ozzy lay listening to the sobs; the prisoner who attempted suicide after discovering that his wife had found someone else to keep her warm at night. It was the relentless sadness of the place; the not-so-silent suffering.

'Ultimately, perhaps my dad did the right thing by letting me go to prison,' Ozzy reflected years later. 'Because it showed me that the criminal life wasn't worth it. For about a week after I came out I was swaggering around thinking I was Jack the Lad. Then it dawned on me that most people rightly thought I was a twat, because I'd been stupid enough to have been caught thieving and sent down for it.'

Back on the street, jobless, friendless and fearing the worst, Ozzy finally got the break which led to 'this great big fucking door opening up in my mind' when he ran into an old pal who told him about a band he was putting together called Approach. Only problem: they needed a singer. 'I'm a singer!' cried Ozzy, having no idea whether he could sing or not. Taken at his word, he was invited to come down to the band's next rehearsal – and to bring his gear. Having even less idea what 'gear' a singer might need, Ozzy somehow persuaded his dad to put his name as guarantor to a hire purchase agreement that allowed his suddenly talented son to acquire a 50-watt PA system with two Shure mikes from George Clay's music shop next door to the Rum Runner nightclub on Broad Street.

'Just holding the mike in my hand, shouting into it, listening to the sound of my own voice booming out of these tiny speakers, I thought, this is it, I've made it,' he laughingly recalled. But all the trials of being in a garage band – infrequent rehearsals, unreliable other members and lack of basic overall talent – soon bred apathy and Ozzy finally stopped showing up altogether. He still fancied himself as a singer, but felt sure he'd never see that dream come true with the inaptly named Approach. Instead, he accepted an invitation to join another start-up outfit named Music Machine, whose bass player, Rosko Gee, would later find fame, briefly, with Traffic. Music Machine at least played live fairly regularly and Ozzy began to take himself more seriously as a singer. Travelling in a tour bus with no brakes, 'The only way we could stop the bus was to run it along the kerb.' The gigs were small, a mix of pubs and youth clubs mainly, but they became regular and the band was making enough money to rent a flat in a slum area of Handsworth which Ozzy also moved into, his first time away from home (not counting prison).

Finding themselves on an ever-decreasing circle of the same gigs, the band eventually lost heart and as soon as one member left the rest folded. Living back at his mum and dad's house, Ozzy stuck a hand-written postcard in a local shop window, advertising the services of 'Ozzy Zig – Singer Extraordinaire – Requires Band – Has Own PA'. As chance would have it, another teenage resident of Aston looking for a leg-up to the big time happened to see it the very next day. His name was Terry Butler – Geezer, to his pals. 'What caught my eye were the magic words: "Has Own PA",' he smiled as he told me the story years later. 'And I saw he lived just round the corner from me, so I went round there…'

But Ozzy Zig wasn't in and so Geezer left his own name and address. 'The next night I was at home and a knock came on the door – and there was Ozzy with this bloody big factory gown on, like this big, brown flared smock thing. He's got that on, a chimney brush over his shoulder, a shoe on a dog-lead and no shoes on. But the thing that really shocked me was his hair – he didn't have any! He had all this stuff on to try and disguise the fact that he was a skinhead. The first thing he said was: "It's all right, I'm growing my hair." I thought, "This bloke's a nut…"'

Geezer – so nicknamed because he used to call everyone *else* 'Geezer' – already had a band called Rare Breed but was looking for a new singer. Ozzy fitted the bill, in so much as 'there weren't anyone else around.' Playing 'psychedelic covers', the band soon fell apart from lack of interest. At which point they merged with the remnants of another local band named Mythology, whose guitarist, Tony

Iommi, and drummer Bill Ward, had been forced to start again after the band had been 'busted for dope.' As Ozzy later told me, 'It was a big thing in them days – you know, Birmingham boys get done with drugs. Big, big news everywhere and they'd had to break the band up. So they were looking for a singer and a bass player, and me and Geezer were looking for a guitarist and a drummer, and that was it.'

Actually, it nearly wasn't it when Iommi discovered who Ozzy Zig really was. 'As soon as I saw him I went, naw, not this bloke,' Iommi told me, 'Because I remembered him from school. At our school, it was pretty…um…you'd give the younger kids a clip round the ear-hole, you know. It was one of those, really. And Ozzy was one of them. He was only a year younger but…they just used to get beaten up.' He chuckled. 'It was one of them.'

'I used to be terrified of him,' Ozzy would tell me. 'When I found out he was the guitarist I was like, oh no! And he was like, "It can't be the same fucking Ozzy I used to know at school, it can't be". You could see it on his face; he thought "No fucking way!" But Geezer smoothed things, I suppose, cos the next thing was we were all playing together in the same band.'

Act 1
Scene Five:

Bad Daddy's Good Girl

As the second and youngest child of Don Arden, Sharon's early life could not have been more different to Ozzy's, yet it was just as strange in its own offbeat way. By the time Sharon Rachel Arden was born on 9 October 1952, Don's early career as a performer in his own right had reached its peak. A song-and-dance man who had become a star of the Variety era – touring with Max Miller and Tommy Cooper and headlining his own shows at London's Palladium – his famous impersonation of the Great Caruso later led to a starring role in the original BBC TV series of the *Black & White Minstrel Show*.

But instead of this leading to a settled home life, as might be imagined, the next few years would find 'the old man' busier than ever as he became sharply aware of his own declining popularity, and that of the Variety scene in general, in Britain at that time. The simultaneous arrival of television and rock'n'roll meant the world was changing around him and suddenly Don was struggling to keep up. Shrewdly judging it better to jump aboard the bandwagon than get left behind, but realising he was too old to reinvent himself as a rival for the new breed of American stars that would take over the pop charts in the mid-fifties, Don set up in business as an agent. His big break came when he landed a contract with the William Morris agency in America, becoming the British and European point of contact for all their artists. This led to an endless stream of tours as more and more US artists began to follow each other across the Atlantic to the lucrative new market Don was then helping develop for them.

In the earliest years of the business, this meant booking acts like Bill Haley, Gene Vincent and Jerry Lee Lewis into a small handful of concert halls in Britain and a much broader selection of US military bases then in operation all across postwar Europe, particularly in Germany. Captive audiences, as Don saw it, that, unable to travel far to shows, he would simply bring the shows to. Operating as a one-man organisation – an expert mimic, he would pretend to be his own female secretary when discussing details on the phone to America – he would expect the whole family to muck in, not least his wife Hope (Paddles to Don, his pet name for her) who had come from a showbiz family herself and therefore knew what was expected. The children, however – David, the eldest by a year, and Sharon – would also have to be brought along as neither was yet old enough for school. As a result, some of Sharon's earliest memories are painful ones of being left with her brother to fend for themselves in strange hotel rooms far from home.

'I spent the first five years of my life going from one military base to another,' she later recalled. 'They'd leave us in the hotel while they did the show and then come back and get us. Nobody would do it today. You'd get arrested.' It was here she demonstrated the determination to make the best of a bad job that would become the dominant characteristic of her later life. As soon as her mother and father had tucked them up in bed and gone out for the night, she would jump out of bed and throw back the covers on David's bed too. Instead of laying in bed frightened and alone, Sharon would persuade her more mild-mannered brother that this was a time for adventure, and the pair of them would spend the next few hours riding up and down in the elevators, pressing the Emergency Stop button and causing havoc for the other hotel guests. Often an irate night porter would try and intervene, calling after them in German, which only caused the children to laugh more and run off. Other times, they would sneak into the hotel kitchen after it had closed down for the night and raid the fridge for drunks and snacks. It was often well past midnight before their parents returned from the gig, by which time both David and Sharon would be tucked back up in bed, looking for all the world like a couple of little angels. It wasn't long, however, before Don began getting complaints from hotel staff about their behaviour and he realised what was going on – and who was largely to blame.

Sharon had always exhibited a rebellious streak, even as a toddler refusing to be held by the hand when she tried to walk. In that respect, where David was quiet and thoughtful and would only lose his temper when pushed to his absolute limit – all qualities inherited from his long-suffering mother, who was older and some said wiser (though never to his face) than Don – Sharon, who could explode at a moment's notice, going from laughter to tantrums and tears within the space of seconds, was very much a chip off the old man's block. Something which Don recognised but which did not make him feel any more kindly towards her. If anything, he did everything he could to try and smooth away the rough edges, sending her to expensive private schools he often couldn't afford in an attempt to try and, as he later put it to me, 'turn her into some sort of fucking lady, with a few manners instead of the evil mouth she always had on her.'

The plan only partly worked, however. While Sharon learnt all about which knife to use and where exactly to plant it in your enemy's back, she was never remotely interested in her studies and quickly became the class clown, cracking jokes and playing pranks in order to pass the time – and to disguise her own basic lack of interest. Something she shared with Ozzy. Meanwhile, with Don's burgeoning business empire increasingly becoming a 24-hour-a-day operation, home life and work blurred into one. Often, Don would bring his famous clients home, and even though Sharon didn't always know who they were exactly, the air of glamour that surrounded them – from their American accents and sharply tailored suits to their exotic-smelling aftershave and hair oil – alerted her to a world her father belonged to far more intoxicating and fun than anything going on at school, no matter how well-run or exclusively appointed. Other times she and David got to glimpse firsthand exactly what it was all about when Don would allow their mother to bring them to shows, allowing them to wander backstage and mingle with the stars. Sometimes this could lead to embarrassing situations, as when David picked up and glanced inside Little Richard's bible – a bizarre tome containing handwritten details in the margins of all of the singer's sexual exploits while on the road.

For Sharon, though, these moments began to represent something far more romantic. 'I can remember being at Victoria Station at midnight, putting Bill Haley on a train to Europe when I was five, because my Dad had him over from America to do a European tour.

And then after that, it was Sam Cooke. I fell madly in love with Sam Cooke at age seven. He used to wear these high-cut matador trousers, and he was built a little bit like Prince, so he had a really neat little body. His cologne was so gorgeous that I could smell where he'd been backstage, and I can remember cowering when he'd come out.' She also recalled being tucked up in bed by Billy Preston – then the teenage keyboard player in Little Richard's band, later guest keyboardist with both The Beatles and the Rolling Stones before embarking on a successful solo career – and playing monopoly with Wee Willie Harris. While it was Gene Vincent who taught her to swim, even though 'his withered leg used to dangle in the water.'

As with their times out on the road in Germany, however, an exotic home life could also have its drawbacks. Living in a large guesthouse in Brixton which her mother Hope would let out some of the rooms of in order to bring in a little extra money, the sort of things Sharon's school friends considered normal – Christmas celebrations, birthday parties, all being home together on Sundays – never gained much purchase in the Arden household. Discouraged from bringing home friends for tea – in order to prevent their 'snooping' parents from also following them around – Sharon didn't even have a favourite dolly or teddy bear as it never occurred to her parents that she needed such things in a life built on constant travel, endless home entertaining and all the other trappings of a life that revolved entirely around Don's seven-day-a-week business dealings.

As Sharon later recalled, 'I hate to use the word "normal" because I don't think it exists, but we didn't have a normal upbringing. There were never birthday parties or Christmas parties as our social life all revolved around work. It was a great way to be brought up, but it was strange.' Not least in the way Don conducted his business. A scrapper since his days exerting his authority over the schoolyard, as he later told me, he modelled much of his way of conducting business on watching Jimmy Cagney movies. Like Cagney, he was short but built to last – quicker to jump over than walk around, as the old saying goes. In his earliest days as a performer, he had been banned from the Variety circuit for beating up a crew member who had dared cross him – prompting a change of name and rejigging of his act. Now as an agent and manager he brooked no challenge to his ways, unafraid to use threats and intimidation, followed up where necessary by actual bodily violence whenever he felt the situation demanded it. These were, as he memorably put it to me, 'The wild west days of the music business and you had to know how to handle yourself.' Again, it was a modus operandi that also spilled over into his home life.

As Sharon said, 'My dad was always threatening people. I was never allowed to bring friends home. It was always business. We didn't know anyone who didn't perform or write or produce. I used to go and stay with my school friend and I couldn't believe the way she lived, how normal it was. Then I'd go back to my house where everything was knocked off and there would be gangsters or some guy running around with a gun. I was surrounded by a lot of violence as a child, a lot of crime. I mean my father was a two-bit hood.'

Sharon, however, was also quick to use whatever means necessary to get her own way. When Don gave her a Jewish Star of David necklace for her ninth birthday, she wore it proudly to school the next day, as she would any piece of jewellery. When, on her way home with David the next day, however, they found themselves surrounded by a gang of older boys, taunting them with racist abuse, rather than David coming to his younger sister's rescue, it was Sharon – diminutive of stature and exceedingly loud of mouth – who frightened them off, screaming abuse at them and threatening them with all sorts of retribution if they dared take another step. Sensing the little she-devil wasn't joking, they backed away nervously, eventually breaking into a run. Sharon and David giggled all the way home. Just like her father had done, Sharon learned early on the importance of always standing your ground, and, as she said, 'putting the fear of God into everyone else.' Something I would see her put into practice to spectacular effect as the years rolled by and the bullies surrounding her grew bigger and even more intimidating.

Equally, whenever she found herself in hot water at school, or decided she'd simply had enough of it there, she had the perfect strategy to deal with it already worked out. She would simply come and perch herself on Don's knee and – knowing which buttons to push – would regale him with made-up stories of all the awful things the rotten teachers had done to her, in order to get him to take her out of the place: a simple but effective method which worked surprisingly well for a long time. 'I knew she was having me on,' he told me, 'but sometimes she was so convincing that I took the bait.' Until one day she went too far and made up a story about one particularly 'evil old witch' who had been picking on her, she said, and treating her unfairly. Outraged, Don threatened immediate retribution.

'I drove down to the school the next morning to confront this bitch who had dared lay a finger on my daughter. When I got there, though, I found that the teacher in question was actually a frail old biddy with a walking stick. She must have been 90 if she was a day! And that was when I realised I'd fallen for one of Sharon's fairy stories again. "She hit me, Daddy! She's evil! Please don't send me back there! No, no, no, Daddy!" I'd have her voice going round in my head all day. One thing about my daughter, she has never lacked persistence – or imagination.'

Because of the flitting from school to school, Sharon made few lasting friends. Even those schools she attended for longer than a few months she remained emotionally detached from, often playing truant, persuading David to join her instead on daytime trips to the cinema or just hanging around the local shops. The only steadying influence she appeared to have at this age came from sporadic visits up north to her paternal grandmother's house in Manchester. Don had grown up in the slums but since his success had purchased a nice semi-detached house for his mother, Sally, in a typically middle-class suburb. Completely unlike her life in London, Sharon adored visiting her grandma's house. Sally would take her granddaughter into town on the bus and they would go shopping together, then take tea at a smart hotel where Sharon would be shown how to sit up straight and behave like a proper, well-bred young lady. It was exactly the sort of old-fashioned outing she never got to enjoy with her own mother and the teenage Sharon relished every moment. She and David also became close to Don's sister Eileen's two children, Cathy and Danny. Cousin Danny was the same age as Sharon; Cathy was considerably younger, but the four kids would play together for hours in Aunty Eileen's back garden.

It was also down to these extended family get-togethers that Sharon first became fascinated with dogs. Nana Sally would often walk Sharon and Danny past the local pet shop and they would all stand and stare through the window at the cute puppies. Soon Sharon was begging Daddy for a cute puppy of her own to take home. Always able to wrap her father round her little finger, wheedling him in the coquettish baby-girl voice she was still using on him as a middle-aged adult, it wasn't long after they returned to London from one such trip that she became the proud owner of two dogs, which she lavished with as much love and attention as though they were her own babies. They slept on her bed and she insisted on taking them with her everywhere she went, including the family's new summer holiday home, a ground-floor seaside flat in Minnis Bay, near Margate in Kent.

Sharon's other passion as a young teenager was becoming a ballerina. To that end, when she was 11 she was enrolled at London's famous Italia Conti stage school. But David was already a pupil there and they fell out as only feuding rival siblings can, and Don soon withdrew Sharon and placed her in a different private school close by. She never quite lost her dream of stardom. When Don booked Hollywood sex symbol Jayne Mansfield to appear in a London show, Sharon was allowed to visit her dressing room and danced around, trying on several of Jayne's much too large but exotically glamorous dresses and shoes, including her eye-catching white leather thigh-boots and tasselled bras.

She was 13 when she again persuaded Don to allow her back to the Italia Conti. By then David was on the point of leaving anyway and so he relented. One of her contemporaries there, now the school principal, was Anne Sheward, who became one of her closest friends. Taking ballet, dance and elocution classes together, Sheward recalls a confident, sharp-tongued girl always determined to get her own way. 'She always had a tremendously big personality,' Sheward remembered. 'She had very good manners, but she was a real character, very quick and very shrewd; she was nobody's fool. Yet at the same time she was very kind. If you were a friend of Sharon's she would stick by you through thick and thin…What you saw was what you got and people liked that about her.'

Despite landing a part in a West End pantomime while she was still at the school, Sharon's potential future success as a professional dancer was always in some doubt, not because of any lack of enthusiasm or talent, but because she was so short (a little over five feet) and heavy, constantly losing out in auditions to the endless thin blondes that were ubiquitous to the ballet world. 'She was always quite hung-up about her weight,' recalled Sheward. 'I can remember her saying: "I've only got to look at a chip and I put on two pounds!" She wasn't huge by any means, but she was heavy and certainly didn't have the long limbs of a typical dancer…'

Dieting didn't help – not even when she discarded the bun from her burger at the local Wimpy Bar in Leicester Square, a favourite hang-out. In the end, she threw in the towel and began frequenting the pub next door to the school, putting on enough make-up to pass for 18 and going there for a pub lunch of beer and sandwiches – hardly the balanced diet of a future ballet queen. But by now Sharon was starting to turn her attention elsewhere.

The mid-sixties found Don reaching new heights in his own career. Still working as a tour promoter for everybody from Chuck Berry and the Everly Brothers to The Beatles and the Rolling Stones, he had also now graduated into full-time artist management. Starting with Gene Vincent and Little Richard, he had gone on to even greater commercial success overseeing the careers, at various stages, of acts like The Animals, the Small Faces, the Nashville Teens, Amen Corner and The Move. Recognised as the most successful – and feared – music entrepreneur in Britain, his kingdom now extended across plush offices in the West End of London and a vast mansion house in the ultra-expensive heart of Mayfair. Don believed that 'money breeds money.' It wasn't enough just to be successful, one had to be seen to be so. To that end, he always made sure that he and wife Hope were always bedecked in the most expensive clothes and jewellery, that his children were ferried to and from school in one of the family's three Rolls-Royces, and that they only ate out in the most exclusive (and expensive) restaurants. It wasn't unusual for him to splash out several thousand pounds on a whim – a piece of antique furniture perhaps or a painting – and give his children anything they wanted. Seventeen-year-old David was allowed to hold lavish parties for all his less well-off friends at the house and have an account for gambling with at a bookmaker's. Not to be outdone, Sharon would also invite her school pals to David's booze-sodden parties, where she made sure she was always the best-dressed, most fashionable-looking girl in the room.

What no one outside the family understood was that Don lived his life as though it were a rollercoaster. When he had it, he was the king at flaunting it. But because of the precarious nature of what was still mostly a cash-rich business – one month a tour would sell-out, the next his latest record was a flop – there were also times when he was strapped for readies. 'I was the girl who moved from Brixton to Mayfair overnight,' Sharon recalled, which was great but came at a price. Her father would 'go from running a huge empire to bankruptcy and back again.' Although they now lived in a huge mansion, often 'we had no phone or electricity because we hadn't paid the bills.' This included, she later claimed, occasions when bailiffs would actually arrive at the house to take possession of enough items to pay off the bills. None of which dented her basic faith in her father's seemingly endless capacity to bounce right back and replace them with bigger and better examples of the things they had just forfeited in so dramatic a style. 'When you are a child and you have someone so strong and so powerful and so successful as your father, you look up to them. Everything he did I thought was right – whatever he said, his opinions, his actions. He was my dad. He was my icon.'

It was not a feeling she shared for her mother, who she was always convinced preferred David. 'It's very hard to admit, but I simply didn't like her,' she confessed years later. 'If I ever hurt myself as a child I'd never run to her for a hug to make it better. There was never that bond between us.'

Having given up on the dream of becoming a dancer, Sharon now begged her father to allow her to work for him. Having already taken on David as an office assistant, he could hardly refuse. Nevertheless, he was disappointed she hadn't finished her education. He was also pragmatic enough to know, however, that when she put her mind to something, like him she wasn't apt to let others stand in her way. He made her the office receptionist. The pay was a mere £12-a-week but she got to ride to work with him every morning in the Rolls.

'It was more like keeping the phone connected, the electricity on and the landlords from kicking us out,' she later recalled. 'If the job hadn't worked out for me, I could have always signed up as a juggler, because that's what I did.' It wasn't long, however, before her strong independent streak reasserted itself and she quit to take a better paid and – she thought – more fun job working behind the counter in a Mayfair bar. She had been there less than a month when she was sacked for consistently mixing the wrong drinks for its well-heeled clientele. Next she became a waitress at the Hard Rock Café but was given her marching orders before she even got started when it became clear she wasn't physically strong enough to carry the trays piled high with drinks glasses and food plates. (Or so she said, anyway, though one suspects she simply didn't fancy it once she realised what hard work it was being on the go all day in such a busy establishment.)

Feeling dejected, she went back to working for the old man. Feeling a failure, she began to comfort eat, and quickly put on weight.

She was no longer just a poor little rich girl, she was a poor little *fat* rich girl. For a while, she even stopped looking in the mirror. 'Cake, fried food, cheeses, anything and everything. Any time I felt a pang of fear, I ate,' she remembered.

But if she thought that was bad, worse was to swiftly follow. A virgin until she was 17, her first sexual encounter – with a good-looking young guitarist in one of Don's bands – left her pregnant. Not close enough to her mother to ask for help, too mortified to approach her father with such news, she didn't know what to do. Then, when she eventually did pluck up the courage to tell Hope, her mother furiously told her she would have to 'get rid of it.' Giving her the name of a local abortion clinic, she sent her there alone the very next day. 'I was terrified,' said Sharon, still upset by the memory years later. 'It was full of other young girls, and we were all terrified and looking at each other and nobody was saying a bloody word. I howled my way through it, and it was horrible. It was the worst thing I ever did.'

It was a long time before she had the confidence to allow another boy into her life – or bed. Instead, she became the fat girl who boys were happy to chat to but only as friends never lovers. When, finally, she did begin again to look for boyfriends it only resulted in a succession of short-lived affairs, purely sexual for the man, heart-breaking for Sharon. It was now, however, that she began to take her work more seriously. With her father now in his mid-forties she felt he was often out of touch with the music scene then beginning to explode in London; the singles-oriented acts like the ones Don specialised in and understood – the 'here today, gone later today' variety as he called them – were now becoming supplanted by a new, long-haired, more flamboyantly dressed breed for whom albums were now the *lingua franca* of their trade, drugs and free love as intrinsic a part of their outlook as the music the new, more freewheeling groups made.

She began to think he needed her help. One of the first of the new breed of bands she twisted his arm about was a group of Brummy 'progressive blues' acts with the provocative handle of Black Sabbath, which she had seen at London's famous Marquee club in 1970. 'I was like, "What the fuck is this?" It was like nothing else.' The next time she noticed they were appearing there she insisted Don came along and saw them too. Suitably impressed, the band was invited to a meeting at the Arden office in Curzon Street. When they arrived, however, their appearance so alarmed Sharon she virtually hid from them. 'I knew they had something from having seen them at the Marquee but in person I just thought they were these awful smelly hippies,' she told me years later. 'I remember they all sat on the floor smoking and they all had really long hair. I was more used to the sort of well-groomed American artists my father usually dealt with. This lot just looked mad to me! The only reason I noticed Ozzy was because he looked like a complete nutter, dressed in what looked like his pyjamas with a water tap round his neck on a piece of string. I really did think he was a lunatic or something.'

Don, who had offered to take them off the hands of the small-time local manager they had and catapult them into the big time, was equally put out but for other, more prosaic reasons. Overawed by his guarantees of turning them into overnight stars and millionaires – 'The sky's the limit!' he roared – convinced he was simply laying it on for effect, and not realising Don really did think and talk like that, they eventually turned him down in favour of an offer from the less high-profile Patrick Meehan and Wilf Pine – as it turned out, two former employees of Don's. The old man was distinctly unimpressed but for once let it go. He'd get his own back one day, he felt sure. And, as usual, he was right.

Sharon, meanwhile, now moved out of her spot on the reception desk and into her father's office, sitting close by him as she started – like her brother – to become a more integral part of the firm. By now the family had moved house again, swapping the palatial Mayfair abode for an even grander property south of the river in leafy Wimbledon. There was a new office in Berkeley Square, too. Despite her unlucky-in-love personal life, Sharon began to enjoy her new status, recognising for the first time what being the daughter of Don Arden actually meant in the British music business of the early seventies. 'I was his princess,' she told me, 'and I could do no wrong. Well, not often anyway. Of course, it all went to my head and I made the most of it. I didn't give a shit.'

Earning good money for the first time and with her own company expense account to use at will, she now had her own Rolls-Royce to ferry her around, never left the house unless she was 'smothered in diamonds, another habit I picked up from the old man who knew how impressed people were with such things' and began living the life to the full. Drink and drugs were all part of the scene in the seventies – as indeed they remain to this day – except that back then it was all still new. The only drug thought to be really harmful was heroin and only lowlifes did that. Mainly, Sharon favoured 'party drug' prescription tranquillisers like Quaaludes; pills which removed those troublesome insecurities and inhibitions and left you feeling euphoric and dizzyingly happy. As she told *Q* magazine years later, 'Oh God, I was the Quaalude queen. And the drinking…'

Meanwhile, Sharon would still bump into those horrid Black Sabbath boys on occasion. To Don's chagrin, David had become matey with Patrick Meehan, who was known for hosting lavish parties. At a New Year's Eve gathering at his London flat to mark the start of 1971, Sharon found herself chatting to Ozzy who, despite his strange garb, she found surprisingly shy and actually very funny. For his part, Ozzy was attracted to Sharon's laugh, a long, throaty chortle that revealed the earthiness that lay just beneath her diamond-encrusted, lady-of-the-manner-like demeanour. High on champagne and each other's company, there was clearly a sexual chemistry between them. Only one problem: for the naive Brummy still on a weekly wage despite his band's roaring success, a girl like Sharon – scary Don Arden's daughter, no less – was way out of his league and, drunk as he was, he knew it.

For Sharon, who knew this was nonsense, there was a more clear-cut reason why they shouldn't get together: the knowledge that Ozzy had a fiancée back in Birmingham named Thelma Mayfair. Having met Ozzy in the Birmingham nightclub where she worked as a cloakroom attendant, they had been together ever since and were due to marry later that year. What's more, Thelma already had a five-year-old son, Elliot, from a previous marriage, and not even Sharon was prepared to start tiptoeing across that minefield. Convinced Ozzy saw her purely as a one-night-stand, she wasn't about to take matters any further, no matter how much he made her laugh. It would be another three years before their paths crossed again and by then both their circumstances had altered drastically.

When Don set up his own record company, Jet Records, in 1974, both Sharon and David became the label's two most important executives – after the old man. It was now that 22-year-old Sharon got her first serious taste of life on the road. Not travelling with her parents this time, but as day-to-day manager of one of the label's first major signings: singer-songwriter Lynsey de Paul. Don had reasoned that being female, Sharon would enjoy a greater rapport with the tiny blonde songstress than he or David would. This time, however, he had guessed wrong. Sharon was at the height of her 'wild child' period, liked to stay up late, get drunk and shit-faced and mainly ate junk food. Lynsey was older, more studious, knew the importance of a good night's sleep, ate sensibly to keep her weight down and was virtually teetotal. The fact the two women were required to share a hotel room at several stops on their first tour together was a recipe for disaster.

Sure enough, it all came to a head one night after a show when Sharon, as usual, decided to sit in the hotel bar drinking rather than follow Lynsey's example and get an early night. As Sharon later recalled, 'This guy had been buying me drinks all night. I staggered back to our room and Lynsey said, "Have you been drinking?" in this prim and proper voice of hers. And I was like "So what if I have?" Her suitcase was open on the floor, so I pulled up my dress and squatted over it. She was like "Are you pissing in my suitcase, Sharon?" And I'm afraid I was.'

Don, who had already decided he didn't like de Paul anyway, didn't bat an eye when Sharon simply walked off the tour the following day. He was less sympathetic when it emerged that Sharon had also recently had a drunken affair with Patrick Meehan – the young buck who had snatched Black Sabbath away from him. Whatever the truth of the matter, when rumours then reached him that Meehan had been showing a videotape he'd made of he and Sharon having sex together, the old man flipped and threatened to kill Meehan. When Meehan then had the misfortune to bump into both Don and Sharon at MIDEM, the annual music-business festival held in Cannes, retribution was swift. 'I went crazy,' Don told me years later. 'My guys jumped in, Sharon jumped in, and the whole thing became like a saloon brawl in a cowboy movie: bottles smashing, chairs flying through the air, the lot.'

When, in 1975, Sabbath sacked Meehan as their manager, it was with a certain Arden-like serendipity that Don immediately moved in and took over their business affairs. But with Sharon by now touring the world acting as tour manager for the even more successful ELO – whose apparently endless sequence of hits throughout the seventies, including 'Mr Blue', 'Livin' Thing' and 'Telephone Line', to name just three, eventually made Don more money than all his other acts put together – her dealings with the Sabbath boys were minimal; her pleasant evening with Ozzy four years before all but forgotten. Instead, when she did get to know them again it was the band's musical leader and taskmaster guitarist Tony Iommi that she turned her attentions to.

With Don now relocating both Jet's head offices and his other business operations to Los Angeles, Sharon and David once again joined him, the whole family moving into the mind-bogglingly impressive mansion legendary film-maker, businessman and recluse Howard Hughes had built and designed for himself 30 years before. It was during their early days at the house that Tony invited Sharon to a Black Sabbath concert at Long Beach arena one night, just a stone's throw from the new offices Don had also now established in Beverly Hills. Though Sharon would deny it for years, it was the start of a relatively brief but, for her, passionate fling with the Sabbath guitarist. She knew he was married but had convinced herself he was genuinely in love with her. As the affair developed over the winter of 1978 she even planned of them setting up home together in LA. In the end, Don told me, 'Tony had to sit her down and tell her straight. "You've got to understand, darling, I love you – but more like a sister." This was at least honest of him, but also about the worst thing he could have said to her.' He added: 'I had to laugh when he told me. It was after her affair with Tony cooled off, though, that Sharon first became interested in Ozzy.'

All of which was true, up to a point. But of course it was never quite that simple. The fact is, Sharon was reaching a turning point in her life. 'Bored shitless,' as she put it, with working for ELO, who, like Lynsey de Paul, did not share her taste for late-night high jinks in hotel bars, she had first turned to, as she put it, very bad behaviour but that, too, had failed to fill the void she now felt opening up within her. She needed more from life than endless travel with 'a load of old age pensioners.' More to the point, she wanted to make her mark outside her father's domain. Her infatuation with Ozzy was no simple rebound from Tony Iommi. Indeed, it was more than a year into her new professional relationship with Ozzy that they first slept together.

No, Sharon had now set her sights higher than a mere love affair with some ready-and-willing rock god. She wanted to be a music business player in her own right. Taking Ozzy off her father's far too busy hands and making him over in her own image, as it were, was suddenly all she could think about. Sensing that if she made a success of it – a gargantuan success of it – it would be her own ticket to...if not stardom then certainly recognition – *real* recognition, not the reflected kind she now enjoyed as 'Don Arden's daughter' – she was determined to give it her everything.

Or as she put it to me years later, 'It was shit or bust for both of us, I knew that going in. Ozzy, bless him, was just glad someone cared, I think. Whereas I knew that if I could get him back on his feet and prove I knew what I was doing, people would have to take me seriously too. We both had a lot to gain – and a lot to lose if we fucked up and got it wrong.'

Act 1
Scene Six:

The Al Capone of Pop

Now that his daughter has achieved far greater worldwide success than even he or his recalcitrant son-in-law could have wished for themselves, he tends to be airbrushed out of contemporary media portraits of the Osbournes. But there's no doubting the place Don Arden holds in their incredible story, or the influential role he played in setting them both on their paths to latter-day glory – if indeed glory it be. Which is a great pity as his story is no less interesting – or bizarre – than theirs. Certainly, it could be argued, without him, there would be no them.

Like almost everybody else that ever knew him, I'd heard about Don Arden long before I ever actually met him. In fact, by the time I finally found myself sitting opposite him, in a pub round the corner from his Park Lane flat in London, in the early weeks of 2002, he was already an old man, suffering from the early stages of Alzheimer's disease. Not that that made him in any way less intimidating to sit and talk to.

You could feel the hush in the pub descend as the well-dressed old gentleman at the corner table began speaking in his overloud voice, the result of an encroaching deafness in one ear. 'I looked him hard in the eye and said: "One false move from you, you bastard, and I'll rip your heart out with my bare hands and shove it down your fucking throat".'

'And, er, how did he respond to that?' I asked nervously. 'He didn't move a muscle,' said Don, turning his ice-cold eyes on me. 'A bloody shame as I would have enjoyed doing that to him. Enjoyed it very much, I would.'

He smacked his lips together and picked up his drink. I glanced around. Everybody else was either madly pretending to read their newspapers or simply staring over at us, astonished. I tried to steer the conversation onto slightly less lurid ground, for the sake of our fellow lunchtime diners.

'But what did you do for fun, back then?' I asked. 'Fun?' roared Don, regarding me as one might an idiot. 'That *was* my fucking fun, don't you see? I'd go in there, smash the place up, bang some heads, then go out and have dinner and champagne at Annabel's. Have a good laugh about it. You have to remember, these people were shit bags! The lowest of the low! They all deserved to die, as far as I was concerned.'

To die? Surely he'd never actually killed anybody, though? 'Well,' he smiled, 'let's just say no bodies were ever uncovered. None that I know of, anyway...' He began to laugh – a long, lusty chuckle that thawed the ice in his pale blue eyes and caused them to twinkle like distant stars. By now, however, both tables either side of us had emptied, and although the pub was as packed as one would expect any lunchtime drinking establishment in Mayfair to be, no one was in any hurry to occupy them. Don Arden, it seemed, had worked his intimidatory magic again.

Magic is the right word too, as so much about Don and the way he was able to manipulate his own image – controlling the way others saw him, reacted to him, and eventually did his bidding – was to do with smoke and mirrors. Obsessed with Hollywood gangster movies, his hero was James Cagney, who he would practise impersonating in front of the mirror. 'Years later,' he told me, 'I used the same techniques before I went into meetings.' He stood up and showed me how he would practise what he was going to say, the threats he would issue, how he would stand and what it would look like. Once, he told me to come at him, as if in anger, in order to show me what he would have done to anyone who dared do such a thing back then. I thrust myself forward, not entirely sure – he was now an old man, after all – and he grabbed my arm and in one easy movement twisted it behind my back before pushing me over and hoisting a kick to my backside. I looked up at him from the floor as he laughed out loud. 'You'll have to do better than that, kid.'

Even his name was an invention. Born Harry Levy in Broughton, Manchester, in 1926, the son of émigré Jews from Russia and Poland, he grew up 'in the ghetto,' he told me, in a house with no electricity and one cold water tap. 'We used to queue up to wash every morning, my father first cos he had to go to work.' The walls of the house were so thin 'when my sister Eileen said her prayers every night the next door neighbours would say "amen".'

Singing in the local synagogue, where his voice was already so strong that he was able to take over from the cantor when he was still in his early teens – unheard of back then – he and mother Sarah – Sal or Sally to the family and their friends – were obsessed with the music hall and would attend shows weekly. Star-struck he dreamed of one day treading the boards himself, perfecting an act reliant on his singing voice and gift for impersonations by doing skits in the playground at school. He lied about his age in order to get his first professional stage job at 14. His mother, who was in on the deceit, signed the forms for him and off he went – the start of what would eventually become a near-60-year career in show business.

It was on the streets, though, that he began to forge the identity that would hold him in such good stead throughout his incident-filled career, both on stage and, more particularly, off it, first as a promoter then artist manager and record company mogul. 'There were so many rats on the street where I grew up, me and the other kids used to have a competition over who could kill the most rats,' he told me. 'I got very good at it, smashing them with rocks. But that wasn't what got me my reputation. It was the first time they saw me come walking down the street whistling, swinging three or four of these dead rats by their tails. It would freak them out. That's when I realised the image of violence was often more powerful than the real thing.'

He wasn't slow to use his fists when he had to, though. 'I also had tremendous strength,' he said. 'It was just a part of me – the Russian part.' To keep in shape he would run 'until I collapsed. I equated physical fitness with mental fitness, and mental fitness with success. There were no gyms to go to because I was travelling all the time, so I would devise other ways of keeping fit,' like running 'with a big, heavy suitcase in each hand.' As a result, he said, 'I was all muscle, no fat. The girls in the show used to call me Tarzan. I'd go to the wings with my shirt off and just a towel round my neck and I'd see guys staring at my physique – they would take one look and not want any part of it.' His propensity for using his fists first and asking questions later soon got him into hot water, however. There was the follow-spot 'schmuck' who used the wrong gel and ruined one of Don's regular impersonations. 'I was only going to rough him up a bit, but he made the mistake of trying to fight back – and that was when I really lost it.' Don beat him up 'then rolled him down the stairs like a bundle of old rags. When he reached the bottom, I jumped on him again. In the end they had to pull me off him…'

More damaging to his own career, however, was the time he took exception to a stage manager named Charlie asking one of the pretty girls waiting outside the Hippodrome in Huddersfield for Don's autograph, 'What do you want that fucking Jew boy's signature for?' Not only was Don angry, he was embarrassed, a potentially deadly combination, certainly for the unfortunate Charlie. 'We were standing in the wings,' recalled Don, 'the curtain was up and there was an act out there doing his stuff. I applied a few good blows to the body and head and he went flying – literally flying – through the air! He ended up laying half on and half off the stage, his head in the orchestra pit. The audience laughed – there was a comedian on stage at the time and they thought it was all part of the act.'

Don wasn't laughing though when the assault resulted in a two-year ban from the northern Variety circuit. At first he thought his career was over but a lucky break with a London-based agent named Julie Golden who specialised in 'Jewish-only' bills landed him a job singing in Yiddish – a throwback to his days singing in the local synagogue, but one that would pay exceedingly well during his so-called two-year ban. By 1948 he was appearing at prestigious London venues like the Palladium and earning up to £350 a week – a fortune for the time.

He hadn't acted so tough though when, in 1944, he had been called-up into the army. 'Terrified' of being sent off to war, he told me how he'd spent the next 18 months faking a 'mystery illness' which kept him near-paralysed and dumbstruck during the week at an army hospital in Southport but 'miraculously' eased up at weekends when he would take part in the army's entertainment corps. More smoke and mirrors successfully applied. When one day one of the nurses on his ward winked at him as she was tucking him up in bed and said, 'I must say, I think you're doing a marvellous job of fooling them all. I can see why you're on the stage,' he said he didn't reply, just looked at her blankly, 'in case it was a trick,' but deep down 'I took it as a compliment.'

The name change from Harry Levy to Don Arden came after he was demobbed at the end of the war. 'It just didn't sound like a star,' he shrugged. 'If I had been a comedian, it would have done fine. But I wanted to be known now primarily as a singer – I was convinced that that would be my passport to the big time – and so I needed a new name.'

It was his agent, Johnny Riscoe, who first suggested it: the 'Arden' from Robert Arden, the Hollywood actor; the 'Don' from another Hollywood star named Brian Don Levy. 'I was quite chuffed when I found out,' smiled Don. 'I used to love Brian Don Levy because he always used to play these semi-gangster types who walked a fine line between right and wrong in order to do what they had to do. I used to love all that as a kid. I understood.' It was as Don Arden that his career really took off, touring the country with an act partly based on his abilities as a singer, partly on his skills as a mimic, impersonating famous figures of the day from Winston Churchill to Mario Lanza, Edward G. Robinson, Bing Crosby, the Great Caruso and – of course – James Cagney. 'Often, it was just a question of getting the right hat' – or in the case of Churchill, the right cigar.

It was also now that he met the woman who was to become his

wife, and mother to his two children. In 1950, he had met and fallen
in love with Hope Shaw, a former acrobat and dancer before the war
under the stage name of Paddy O'Shea. Nicknamed Paddles by Don,
Hope came from a well-known show business family in Ireland where
her father was a famous tenor and her mother, Dolly, had led a troupe
of dancers named the O'Shea Girls. By the time Don met her, Dolly
had retired and opened a guesthouse in London, known for putting
up travelling showbiz types like him, then still based in Manchester.
Morecambe and Wise were regular guests there, as was Tommy
Cooper, which was how Don had heard about the place.

When Dolly's daughter Hope turned up with a group of mutual
friends backstage at one of Don's London shows he was instantly
smitten, he said – despite the fact that she was nearly 10 years older
then him and already a mother of two children from a previous
marriage: Richard and Dixie. The fact that she came from a showbiz
family meant she wasn't like the girls he usually went for and the
couple embarked on a whirlwind romance, ending with their
'quickie' marriage just a few months later at Lambeth Register
Office. It was April 1950 and Don had never been so happy before;
happy to lend his name to Richard and Dixie too. The only blot on
the horizon was Don's mother, who he had deliberately not invited
to the wedding, nor indeed even mentioned Hope to until their
second child, Sharon, was born two years later. The reason: Paddles
wasn't Jewish. Worse, she was older – considerably older by the
standards of staid fifties' Britain. The fact that she was also a divorcee
with two kids put her completely beyond the pale for a proud
Yiddisher mother like Sally. Predictably, she was 'furious' when Don
finally let the cat out of the bag, unable to keep quiet the news of
David's birth in 1951, refusing even to meet her son's wife or even

come and see the grandson she now had. 'It wasn't until after Sharon was born that my mother finally accepted the fact that I now had a wife. Then they became firm friends.'

By now, Don, Paddles and all four kids were living in a large rambling Victorian house in Angell Road, Brixton, south London, leased from Winifred Atwell, the pianist and a showbiz acquaintance of the couple's. The house had seven bedrooms spread over four floors and Don and Paddles made use of every spare inch of space, primarily as a home for the family, but also as an office for Don and a business for Paddles, who would rent out the spare rooms to other showbiz people.

With Don now turning his attention full-time to working behind the scenes as an agent, home and work life blurred into one long song-and-dance of its own. 'It was 24-hours-a-day, seven-days-a-week, 52-weeks-a-year,' he told me. 'It had to be, there was only me and Paddles trying to stay on top of things. Every other bugger was trying to either do us down or steal from us.' But if the work was relentless, these were all Don's Great Days. 'It was like the Wild West back then, and I was the fucking sheriff.' The days when he first brought American rock'n'rollers to Britain like Jerry Lee Lewis ('A real redneck'), Little Richard ('A pervert but I loved him') and Gene Vincent ('A fucking lunatic, much worse than Ozzy or anybody you've got now'). Or when he ran the Star Club in Hamburg ('Any trouble at all and I would knock 'em out and have 'em thrown unconscious into the gutter') where he also encountered The Beatles ('I didn't think much of 'em, not compared to Richard or Gene').

Clearly, his musical judgement wasn't always failsafe. But he learned quickly and when The Beatles changed the music business overnight Don was ready to change with it, signing first The Animals then the Nashville Teens and, later, the Small Faces and The Move,

Ozzy (far left) and Black Sabbath, 1971. Forming the band was 'the quickest way out of the fucking slums.'

Ozzy on stage in America with Randy Rhoads, 1981. When they first met, Ozzy thought 'Randy was so pretty he was a chick.'

Sharon and Ozzy on their wedding day in Maui, 4 July 1982. Ozzy spent the night passed out in the corridor outside the wedding suite.

Sharon and Ozzy at home in London, 1983. Friends held a betting school on how long the marriage would last.

Ozzy and Tony Iommi on stage with Black Sabbath at Live Aid, Philadelphia, 1985. Ozzy was so fat he thought he looked 'like Mama Cass at a gay party!'

Ozzy at the height of his solo stardom in the late 1980s. 'If it hadn't been for Sharon I would have been out selling hotdogs.'

Sharon with her father Don Arden, reconciled after a twenty-year 'war' in 2002.

'The most dysfunctional TV family since the Simpsons!' And the most successful. Sharon, Ozzy and Kelly in the spotlight, 2008.

to name just a few. 'None of them had a clue what to do till I came along,' he boasted. And there was some truth in that. It was Don who paid for The Animals to leave Newcastle and tour the country on the back of the recording he had paid for them to make of a song called 'House of the Rising Sun'. And despite their later claims that he ripped them off, it was Don who paid for the large London house the Small Faces lived in, along with the chauffeur-driven Jag they rode around town in and accounts at all the smart Carnaby Street shops they bought all their clobber in. It was also Don who handpicked their breakthrough hit, 'Sha La La Lee'. 'I wanted something like "Do Wah Diddy" by Manfred Mann which was then Number One so I went to my mate Kenny Lynch to write it. The band hated it but it brought them massive success. Then they were all kissing my feet.'

It was also in the sixties that Don's hard-man reputation really took off. Beloved by his artists who he would always 'treat like royalty' and loathed by the hangers-on that, as he saw it, 'leeched off the artists, sucking their blood dry,' he took a special dislike to drug dealers and bootleggers – sellers of unofficial group merchandise, often outside the venues where the artists were appearing. The former because 'I'd never taken drugs myself and couldn't understand why anyone else would want to, it was pure poison and you ended dead or worse than dead.' The latter because: 'These fuckers were basically stealing money as sure as if they'd had their hands in the artists' pockets – and mine. I wasn't going to stand for that!' Having 'assembled an impressive array of nasty-looking characters around me: "security" staff that I always had on standby,' his solution was, he told me, 'to tackle both problems the same way – go in hard and hit them where it hurts.'

Don's gang included Peter Grant, a 6ft 5in (1.96m) 20-stone (127kg) giant who had begun as Don's 'driver' before graduating to tour-managing Gene Vincent – and who would later find his own special notoriety as the feared Don-like manager of Led Zeppelin; Patrick Meehan, a former film extra and bouncer – and father of Patrick Junior, who would later manage Black Sabbath and fall into Don's black books over his brief affair with Sharon; Stan Simmon, who was 'another good guy to have around in a tight spot'; and one particularly colourful character who went by the name of Mad Tom.

'We never went looking for trouble but I made it clear I wouldn't hesitate to act if any started, however big or small the problem. In fact, I found that if you dealt with the small stuff decisively it helped prevent the big stuff from happening. People would look at how severely you dealt with a relatively minor incident and wonder what the hell you would do if something really serious occurred.'

Minor incidents included 'chinning' a music journalist who had made the unfortunate error of 'bad-mouthing' Don to his son, David. When the unfortunate hack had the temerity to land on one of Don's most cherished cars, a white Chevy Impala, 'I hit him again for being a cheeky shite and denting my car!'. Or the time Don had some of the boys kidnap Small Faces' producer Glyn Johns in the middle of the night and tie him to a tree on Barnes common. Johns had 'a big mouth' Don decided and needed to be 'taught a lesson he'd never forget.'

Major incidents, like dealing with bootleggers, would be left to Mad Tom. 'At first, he was just one of my guys but he developed such a good routine that he was able to frighten most of them off all on his own.' So good, in fact, Don would follow him outside to watch. 'Tom would go up to them and say, "My boss says you've got to fuck off." Often they'd just look at him and start laughing. They thought he was a bit backward, which I suppose he was. But he was built like

Frankenstein's monster and he'd soon wipe the smile off their faces. He would ask them again. If they hadn't responded sufficiently after the second request he simply picked the nearest one up and brought him down on his knee, snapping his back like a twig. Sometimes you heard the crack. Then he would pick them up again and toss them into the gutter. Mad Tom used to shell 'em like peas. Then we would "confiscate" all the merchandise they had been pushing and – if it was any good – flog it ourselves inside the hall.'

The most famous incident involving Don and his 'boys' – and one that has since passed into music biz folklore – was when he hung fellow impresario Robert Stigwood out of a window by his feet, for daring to try and take over as manager of the Small Faces. Enraged, Don took '10 of the biggest, ugliest-looking creatures you've ever seen' with him to Stigwood's Cavendish Square office, marched in, ordered some of his men to 'take over the phones' so no one could call the police, then walked in and confronted Stigwood personally. 'I lifted him out of his chair and dragged him over to the balcony. He was crying, "No, Don! No, Don!" I stuck his head over the edge of the balcony rail and said, "You see that fucking street down there? Well, that's where you're going the next time you fuck with me!" At which point I was going to give him a couple of digs maybe and leave it at that. Job done.' But it wasn't over yet. Don's crew had 'decided to play a little gag on me' and one of them shouted, 'Fuck next time! Let's sling him now!' At which they all rushed forward and lifted Stigwood up and carried him to the edge of the balcony and began swinging his body as if to throw him off. 'Stigwood must have gone into shock because his body went completely limp,' Don laughingly recalled. 'It was as if he'd died: everything just left him at once and he shit himself. He wore cowboy boots and the shit was squelching down his jeans into them. The stink was so terrifying the boys had to drop him. We left him there on the floor, lying in his own ordure, not even moving. He never bothered me again.'

A less famous but even more terrifying occasion involved Clifford Davis, who Don was in dispute with over the management – again – this time of The Move. Only Don didn't bring his boys with him on this occasion; he was so angry, he said, he just ordered his driver to take him straight to Davis' office. When he arrived he found Davis seated with his feet up on his desk, nonchalantly smoking a large cigar. After some initial banter of the 'I know where you live' variety, Don lost patience and went for Davis where he sat. 'I took the cigar out of his mouth with my right hand and grabbed him by the back of the head with my left…Then, holding him tight, I drilled the lit end of the cigar into the middle of his forehead. He struggled of course but I was too strong, too intent upon my work, and I held him there for a long time until he went limp. I wanted to see if I could actually penetrate his forehead with that thing. Eventually the crushed embers of the cigar fell down between his knees and burned a hole right through his trousers and into the leather chair he was sitting on. I started to laugh…'

He told me it made him feel 'so good' that afterwards he dismissed his driver and walked home – whistling. Later that same evening he celebrated by treating his staff to champagne at his favourite nightclub, Annabel's. 'We'd all piss ourselves laughing as I told them the story,' he remembered. 'They were great days to be alive!'

Of course, such stories spread throughout the music business like wildfire. The message clear and simple: you didn't mess with the Don. 'Looking back now, I suppose it could be a double-edged sword,' his son David would tell me. 'It meant that a lot of people were so scared of the old man they didn't want to have any dealings with him whatsoever. On the other hand, it meant he tended to get his way own a lot whenever we were doing deals with record companies and people like that.'

With David joining his father's business full time in the early seventies, father and son soon developed what David now calls their 'good cop, bad cop routine.' For example, if ever Don was having trouble getting a big enough tour budget or album advance, perhaps, from a record company executive, he and David would arrange a meeting with said exec at his office, during which Don would deliberately lose his temper and start smashing the place up, turning desks over and issuing violent threats at the top of his voice. Then he would storm out, leaving a rueful-looking David to pick up the pieces. Softly-spoken, mild-mannered David had perfected his good cop act almost as well as his father's bad cop. 'I'd say to them: "Look, I can stop this for you, if you like. But you'll have to help me". By which point they'd be so rattled they were ready to give me anything just to stop the old man coming back. I'd walk out of there with twice the figure we'd been hoping to get in the first place. Then when I got downstairs the old man would be waiting for me in the car and we'd both have a good laugh about it as we drove back to the office.'

Aware of his larger-than-life image, Don began playing on it in other ways, too. Like the rumour that did the rounds for decades that he always carried a gun with him wherever he went. In fact, it wasn't true – though he had carried a gun into meetings and on other occasions at various intervals over the years. Almost always, though, for the effect such an act would have. 'Sometimes I would just lay it on the table at meetings. It had a wonderful way of focusing everybody's minds,' he told me with a broad smile. There was even a famous invitation card for the annual Jet Records Christmas party one year that boasted a picture on the front of Don standing in front of a Christmas tree holding a gun, with the words HERE'S AN OFFER YOU CAN'T REFUSE emblazoned across it.

By the mid-seventies, Don was now not just one of the most successful rock managers in the world – overseeing ELO, Ozzy and Black Sabbath, Roy Wood's Wizzard (famous for No. 1 hits like 'See My Baby Jive' and 'I Wish It Could Be Christmas Everyday') and several others – but also one of the biggest promoters – bringing not just music stars to Britain and Europe but now branching out to include names like then world heavyweight boxing champion Joe Frazier. He was also about to become head of one of the most successful record companies, Jet Records, featuring a galaxy of talent, including its first major signing Lynsey de Paul, whose first Jet single, 'No, Honestly', became the company's first Top Five hit.

When he decided to move his operations full time to Los Angeles, it was both the fulfilment of a lifetime's work and a childhood dream come true. 'I'd dreamed of living in Hollywood since I was a kid sitting in the dark at the pictures,' he said. 'To find myself finally doing it at the age of 50 was amazing. Everything I could ever have wanted and a whole lot more.'

Living in the famous old Howard Hughes mansion in Hollywood, throwing lavish celebrity-filled parties in the atrium, Don's best friends now included Cary Grant and Tony Curtis. Harvey Weinstein, who would go on to form the mega-successful Miramax film company, was another acolyte. 'He was like a son to me'. It was through his friendship with Grant that Don also became involved with the Republican Party of Ronald Reagan, invited to fund-raisers and later, when Reagan became president, to the White House itself, where Grant – an old friend of the President's from his Hollywood movie days – went out of his way to introduce Don to him.

But if becoming a part of the American establishment held huge appeal for the former song-and-dance man from Manchester, it was his much longer-standing association with another old American institution that he was still showing off about when I got to know him a quarter of a century later: the American Mafia. Specifically, his friendship with Joe Pagano, then head of one of the five big Mafia 'families' in New York. 'Decent, family people,' Don called them. Maybe so. But people that had also reportedly been connected to more than 150 'contract' killings over the years. The first time they met, Don told me, it was because he had forcibly resisted an attempt by the Pagano family to take over the management of ELO. Not realising who he was dealing with yet, Don had accused Pagano of being 'a fag' – not a term to endear him to a Mafia crime boss.

Pagano was intrigued, however, by anyone bullish enough to stand up to him and invited Don to a lunch. 'It was a place on 77th Street and Second Avenue, a lovely, old-fashioned, family-run Italian bar, just like you see in the movies,' Don recalled. In London, he had always enjoyed the company of powerful hard-men such as Charlie Kray, brother of Ronnie and Reggie. But this was something else. Don took David with him to the meeting with Pagano and when they walked in 'they were all there, these guys in their suits. And in the middle of it all was this wonderful little man, old but sharp with it, with the little hat, smoking a cigarette. It was all very friendly and charming…David and I loved it. We both loved Mob movies and this was almost like being in one.'

Having apologised for any 'misunderstandings', the Ardens and the

Paganos parted friends that day. 'It was all kisses on the cheek and slaps on the back. "Next time you come to New York," said Joe, "let me know and I'll send my car for you." And he did – big limo I think he must have had specially built. It was probably bulletproof.' It was the start of a cosy relationship that would endure for decades. According to Don, despite all the true-life Mob stories 'the Joe Pagano I got to know in the late-seventies and eighties was one of the most charming, intelligent and genuinely caring men I have ever had the pleasure to know. What he did or didn't do in his business – well, that was up to him. We were civilians, so it didn't affect us. Those old-time Mobsters had a code about things like that and, if you were their friend, they really looked after you.'

In return, whenever ELO played New York, Joe and his family were gifted as many tickets and VIP passes as they desired, several hundred if necessary. They would also be honoured guests at the after-show parties. 'I discovered that the greatest thing in the world to a Mafioso was to be able to step out of those surroundings for a while and go out and have dinner or a party with some straight people.' And of course they would know how to show their appreciation. 'The best-dressed people in the city…lined up, waiting to kiss my hand.'

Included in such line-ups would be longstanding Pagano family members such as Big Frankie, Bobby Bomps, and – most notoriously – Joe's son, Danny Pagano. David later told me how, over the years, Don actually became closer to Danny – who could be 'a bit more of a head-case like the old man' – than he was to Joe, who, conversely, David was closer to in temperament. David recalled how Joe once remarked: 'The trouble with your father, he wants to kill everybody.' Danny Pagano, who later served six-and-a-half years in jail, 'was tough,' Don told me admiringly, 'I loved him as if he were my own son.' The child that would eventually cause Don the most headaches, however, was not his son – real or metaphorically adopted – but his daughter, Sharon.

Always a daddy's girl, Don both 'spoiled' Sharon as a little girl – private schools, expensive clothes and jewellery, foreign travel – yet failed to be there for her at several crucial junctures – birthdays and other important family events, most notably when he was kept in the dark about her pregnancy. With 'normality' a concept completely alien to their home life, in the end the best he could do for her was to show her how the world – his world – worked, from the nitty-gritty of cash deals done in the dead of night to the high-gloss finish of multimillion-dollar contracts, and, not least, the 'hands on' way he had of dealing with anyone who dared stand in his way.

As a result, he told me, 'People said I was a handful but I was nothing compared to my daughter.' From her choice of boyfriends – 'Sometimes I thought she picked them just to wind me up' – to her cavalier approach to money; most especially, his money. He recalled several outlandish examples. Like the time in 1977 when he was embarrassed having dinner in New York one night with his wife and some friends. When he went to pay the bill with his family credit card, he was taken to one side by the maître d' who told him he had someone from American Express on the phone who needed to speak to him. Furious, Don grabbed the phone ready to give whoever was on the other end of the line hell, only to be informed that Am-Ex had thought it prudent to check with him in person first before authorising any more payments on the card as so much money had already been charged to the account in the previous 24 hours.

'What the fuck are you talking about?' roared Don. 'He quoted me a figure somewhere in the region of $300,000 and I nearly collapsed!

"I haven't bought anything worth $300,000!" I bellowed. "No, sir," he said. "But it appears your daughter has..."' Don looked at me, still aghast all these years later. 'She had spent the entire amount on jewellery!' There was one item for something like $175,000 from Van Cleef, he remembered: one for $75,000 from Tiffany's, and one for about $50,000 from Cartier – all bought in the space of a single afternoon.

Hurrying back to his hotel that night he immediately called Sharon on the phone and demanded an explanation. 'Oh, Daddy,' she said, in that little-girl-lost voice she always used on her father to get her own way, 'I was so bored, I had to do something...' Adding insult to injury, Don discovered that not long after, Sharon had blithely gifted the $175,000 necklace to her pal, Hollywood actress Britt Ekland – also then signed to Jet – who then gave it to her children's nanny! 'I nearly burst a blood vessel,' sputtered Don.

Another time, on tour with ELO, Sharon somehow contrived to leave her leather jewellery case in the limo on her way from the airport to the hotel. Don recalled how she spent several hours trying to track down the driver but all to no avail. 'Then it was time to go to the show and so she promptly forgot about it. I'm talking about a collection of jewellery then worth in the region of $750,000 – and this was 25 years ago.' Once again, however, Sharon's reaction was nonchalant. 'Don't worry, Daddy,' she smiled sweetly, 'It's all insured.' But when Don reminded her of the incident a couple of weeks later, checking to see what progress had been made with the insurance claim, she simply shrugged. 'Oh, yeah! I must do that...' His face was like thunder as he recounted this.

It wasn't until she began working with Ozzy, he said, that she finally grew up and began to take life more seriously. 'Well,' he chuckled darkly, 'she had to then, didn't she? I mean, one of them had to!' His face darkened again, though, at the suggestion that it was Sharon who single-handedly turned Ozzy's career around after his sacking from Black Sabbath in 1979. 'Sharon always gets the credit for this but people forget that it was me who was his manager, me that decided to ditch Sabbath and stick with Ozzy, and me that funded the whole launch of his solo career.'

Certainly, it was clear how much affection Don had for Ozzy. 'He was a one-off,' he smiled. 'Imagine, though, what it was like having him as a house-guest for a year, especially in those days when he was still all over the place? That's what I needed Sharon for, to help us all cope with just having him around.' He shook his head at the memory. 'People got up and left the room when they saw him coming. Thankfully, Ozzy has always been a funny guy, which is why I always ended up forgiving him.'

Still at the height of his drink and drug taking, Ozzy was certainly a challenge. 'Mainly, it was the booze,' said Don. 'He'd start with one, next thing he'd pissed himself and fallen down the stairs and set fire to the house! He was one of those – a walking accident waiting to happen.' What saved him, in Don's eyes, was that 'Ozzy was never evil. He doesn't have a bad bone in his body. He only ever looked to have fun when he was with me.'

The fun began to pale, however, when it became clear to Don that there was more to Sharon's relationship with Ozzy than mere business – especially when that relationship now appeared to threaten that business. He recalled how Ozzy 'did a disappearing act' on the eve of his first British tour as a solo artist in November 1980. Ozzy and Sharon's affair was no longer a secret, even to Don, and when Ozzy's wife Thelma also got to hear of it, 'all hell broke loose.' In fact, Ozzy had immediately gone on a bender before returning to his own family home in Birmingham and throwing himself at the mercy of Thelma. He had also shaved all his hair off. 'I thought: "Is this guy deliberately trying to ruin me?"'

Don followed Ozzy back to Birmingham, where he did everything he could to calm Ozzy down and reassure Thelma that the affair with Sharon was a one-off that had now run its course. That he would personally ensure it never happened again – as long as Ozzy promised to pull himself together and return to the tour.

Then, just as it seemed Don's words had done the trick, Ozzy leaned over and in front of Thelma told Don straight: 'It's as simple as this. I love your daughter and I want to marry her!' He laughed as he told me the story. He didn't know who was more shocked, he said, Thelma or him. Before the meeting, the worst that could happen, he thought, was that he might not be able to persuade Ozzy to come back and restart his career. 'It never crossed my mind I might be inheriting a son-in-law!'

He wondered if Sharon really knew what she was letting herself in for, then conceded that after living under the same roof as Ozzy for several months she probably did. He recalled the nights when he would awaken to strange sounds coming from outside his bedroom door. When he went to investigate there would be Sharon 'struggling down the hall with a double-bed mattress on her back. "What the fuck are you doing?" I cried. She didn't even look at me. "Piss!" she screamed.' Ozzy had reached that stage of his alcoholism where he would routinely wet the bed every night.

And yet, despite their obvious differences, they shared many of the same characteristics too, he said. 'They were both quite out-rageous individuals when they wanted to be, didn't care what anybody else thought about anything.' He recalled another occasion on an early Ozzy tour when Sharon had rowed with the hotel manager over the bill, screaming at him: 'You fucking cocksucker! Fuck you, baby! I'm out of here!' Then hitching up her skirt and urinating in a large plant pot in the lobby. 'In the end, they had to call the police to get her to leave.'

The 'real trouble' only started, though, Don insisted, after they decided they were going to be a couple. At first, he tried to be philosophical about it, he said. 'When two people are in love like that, it doesn't really matter what anyone else thinks. All we could do was wish them well and wait to see what happened next.' What he hadn't bargained for was that Ozzy having an affair with Sharon was a situation that would lead to 'such dire consequences that she and I would become such bitter enemies that for years she would actually tell her own children I was dead…'

Act 11

Death, Drugs, Hollywood Madness!
Wives, Children & a Fat Joan Collins!
Murder, Drunkenness & the Sins of the Father!
Or: What Did Daddy do in the War, Mummy?

Scene One:

The Big Bong Theory

By the start of the nineties, Los Angeles had become a second home for me. So, too, Ozzy and Sharon, who had kept the big old mansion they'd splashed out £2.5 million for in England, but now decided that LA was the place to be. They'd been going back and forth for years of course but for me it was still a fairly new experience: not the city, which I'd been exploring for a decade or more, but actually calling the place home.

'Everybody's here now anyway,' Sharon had laughingly declared one day as we sat having yet another lunch by yet another swimming pool. 'What would you want to go back to cold, boring old England for?' She said it with her most coquettish smile and I nodded my head in agreement. It wasn't that 'everybody' was here now literally, of course, just the ones that mattered most to Sharon – i.e. the main movers and shakers of the music business, this still being at least a decade before she and Ozzy would exchange that weird world for the even more glitteringly arse-kissing and infinitely better-paid universe of reality TV.

She certainly seemed to be in her element as we sat in the shade, enjoying our iced tea and mineral water, me trying not to spill it down my front as I laughed out loud at her wonderfully indiscreet stories of music biz infelicity and breathtakingly selfish derring-do. The one about the record company exec who only signed bands who 'take it up the arse'; the ageing Lothario singer, new in town, whose fiancée was well known back in her Hollywood High groupie days for 'fucking Alsatians'; the girl singer who only shacked up with guys who knew how to 'give her a black eye'; the time on tour when Sharon woke up in the middle of the night to find Ozzy had brought a groupie back to their hotel room and put her in the bed next to where she was sleeping. 'What did you do?' I gasped. 'I fucking whacked her round the head!' she roared with laughter. 'It was no use blaming Ozzy. He was too fucking out of it to know what he was doing. She should have known better, though – actually climbing into the bed next to me!' It's a wonder I managed to finish my Caesar salad at all.

Of course, there was a lot more to Sharon than knowing who's fucking who and what's paying for what. Behind the funny stories and eye-rolling innuendo, there was a big brain working overtime, a pulse of steel and a mouth that could – and did – maim at will. Only a few weeks before I had witnessed her – as she put it – 'tearing a new arsehole' into a photographer friend who had committed the heinous crime of repeating rumours we had all heard and repeated to each other – that Sharon had had a fling with a certain musician – but which only the hapless photographer had been unfortunate enough to have Sharon find out about.

We were backstage at Irvine Meadows, a huge outdoor amphitheatre on the outskirts of LA used to house performances by big name rock acts like Ozzy himself or, in this case, the British rock band Whitesnake. We were standing in the green room – a specially designated area backstage where all the VIP guests could mingle – chatting amiably when the photographer showed his face. Spotting her prey, Sharon immediately lit into him. It was like a scene from an old-fashioned cowboy movie where everyone, including the piano player in the striped shirt, stops what they're doing and the room goes deathly quiet – all except for the loud and rapidly getting louder voice of the Killer as he bears down on his Victim, with Sharon very much in the role of the Killer.

'You fucking piece of shit!' She roared at the white-faced lensman. 'You dirty motherfucker! How *dare* you spread fucking rumours and lies about me!'

No one else in the room knew where to look. The photographer was no stranger to any of us, least of all Ozzy, who had worked with him for years. Like the rest of us, however, Ozzy merely stood there silently, waiting for the storm to pass, staring at his feet. Afterwards, the photographer was close to tears. A bizarre sight as rock photographers as a breed are hardly known for their sensitive sides, the development of a particularly thick skin being an essential requirement of the job. What's more, this particular snapper had a reputation for being one of the hardest in the biz. But he was so upset he couldn't even go on and finish shooting the rest of the show. An old friend, I drove with him back to the hotel, commiserating. The fact that he had been telling tales, as it were, didn't seem to matter as he was hardly the only one. The rest of us were just glad it wasn't us that Sharon had found out about.

Now, over lunch, however, when I brought his name up, Sharon merely smiled and said how much she liked working with him. 'But…the other night?' I enquired tentatively. 'Oh, that,' she giggled.

'That's over, done with. I said my piece and now it's all forgotten as far as I'm concerned. No, if he wants to come and do some shots of Ozzy that's absolutely fine.'

When I conveyed this news to our mutual friend, there was relief all round. As a signifier of how the music business works – or certainly how the Ardens worked, as I had discovered – it was a fairly typical example. Within months, he would be back in the bosom of the Osbourne family, snapping away to his heart's content. The message was clear: like her father, Sharon was definitely not someone you would wish to tangle with; unlike her father, she didn't bear grudges. Happy to forgive, if never to entirely forget: that was her motto. Or so it seemed back then.

One wondered what Ozzy made of it all. Ask him and you'd get a different answer every time. 'She saved my life,' he would repeat like a mantra, that far away look in his eye, like a child contentedly sucking his thumb in his pram. Other times, he'd look at me with the anguished face of that same child doing a poo in his nappy and grizzle: 'I can't stand it. She's driving me fucking nuts!'

Before one could answer, it always had to be borne in mind first which mode Ozzy was currently in. That is to say, was he on the wagon or off it – again? When Ozzy was on the wagon – which he seemed to be only occasionally, though he never stopped talking about it – then Sharon could do no wrong. Even when he was decidedly off the wagon, which he was almost every time she turned her back, even then he could be relied on to sing her praises. And why not? She really had, after all, not only rebuilt his career after the disastrous sacking from Black Sabbath, she had single-handedly kept him at or near enough to the top of the tree ever since, no matter what obstacles had come their way, and there had been more than their fair share. Sometimes, however, just occasionally when no one else was around and he was feeling particularly hard done by – often when he knew he'd have to get up to go to work in the morning – he would let rip. What a bummer it was having your 'old lady' manage you. How he'd 'never fucking get to see her any more, and when I do all she fucking talks about is work, work, work.'

Not really wanting to hear all this but at the same time not wishing to be a disagreeable guest and start arguing the toss, I would simply sit there nodding along, making suitably sympathetic noises, waiting for an opportunity to change the subject. Like guys do when they get together and one of them makes the fatal error of slipping into a rant about their wife/girlfriend/ex/current/whatever. So much safer and more fun to talk about almost anything else, after all, right? Right, Ozzy?

This is something I learned the hard way during the recording sessions for what would become Ozzy's 1991 album, *No More Tears*. Although they had already made up their minds to move back to LA more or less permanently, he and Sharon hadn't bought a new home yet, so while Sharon stayed in England taking care of business from her office in London – still her main place of business back then – Ozzy was temporarily holed-up in a small apartment in West Hollywood a couple of blocks up from the hotel I was then staying in. Having interviewed him one afternoon for yet another magazine piece, he invited me over to his apartment that night to 'hang out'. Not entirely sure which Ozzy I would be hanging out with – on or off the wagon Ozzy – I wasn't sure I was really up to it. A quiet evening with a bottle of wine in front of the TV was what I'd originally had in mind. If Ozzy was on the wagon that would mean no wine for either of us. I tried to wriggle out of coming to see him but he wasn't having it. 'Come on,' he said, 'Sharon's away and I'm fucking bored.' He looked at me with those big, permanently startled eyes and I realised suddenly he wasn't kidding. He was bored and something else, too: lonely. Oh, all right then. But I wouldn't be staying late, I warned him…

I arrived at his apartment block at about eight that evening but he wasn't answering his buzzer. At first, I thought maybe he'd forgotten I was coming and gone off somewhere else. Typical! I was just about to give up and go home when the lobby door opened as someone else left the building. I dived in before the door could close again and rode the lift up to his floor. When the doors opened I could hear loud music blaring out from somewhere. As I searched for the apartment number he'd given me the music grew louder – and louder. I realised as I found his door that it was Ozzy's apartment the music was coming from. No wonder he hadn't heard the door buzzer. You could hardly hear yourself think. And there was something else on top. A voice; *his* voice, I realised. He was singing. What was he doing that for? I had never heard Ozzy actually *singing* before. Not unless he was on stage, obviously, or in the vocal booth in the studio. What the fuck was going on?

I waited for the minutest break in the music then knocked loudly on the door. This time he heard me, or someone did. There was what sounded like a running sound then the door flung open before me. Standing there was some kid I'd never seen before, about 18 years old, maybe, his hair long, his eyes wide with what looked like shock. Behind him, perched on the edge of the couch sat Ozzy. 'Who is it?' he called out. 'Dunno, some guy,' the kid yelled back. 'Well, tell him to come in!' shouted Ozzy as the music kicked in again.

I thought it might be one of the musicians on the album. Sharon was always hiring younger and younger hotshots for Ozzy's backing group. Then the song finished, Ozzy caught sight of me and got up to greet me. 'Allo mate,' he said, 'How's it going?'

'Fine,' I said. 'What are you doing?'

'It's me new album, I'm just playing some of it to…um…' He looked across at the kid, 'What's yer name again, mate?'

'John,' said the kid. Or maybe it was Ron, or Lon, you really couldn't hear. Seeing his opportunity, the kid made his move, grabbing his jacket and spluttering his farewells. It was plain he was in a hurry to leave.

'Gee, Ozzy, man, thanks, man, that was awesome, man. And thanks for the autograph, too! But I gotta go, man. But, gee, you know, thanks very much! And nice meeting you too, sir,' he said, turning to me, briefly. His face was white and he looked shaken, like he'd just been pulled from the railroad tracks as a big freight train bore down on him.

'Yeah, awright then mate, cheers,' said Ozzy as the kid sped past me and out the door.

'Who was that?' I asked as the door slammed shut behind him.

'I dunno. Some kid who was waiting outside for an autograph. He told me he'd been waiting there all afternoon, so I thought he might like to hear a bit of the album, you know? I think he liked it as well. Here, let me play you a bit…'

I sat down on the couch as he plonked himself next to me and turned the tape machine back on, full blast. Just as he had with the freaked-out kid, he sat there playing his tape and singing along at the top of his voice, treating me and what must have been everyone else on that floor of the building to the half-finished songs from his next album. Once I got used to the volume, I noticed that some of the songs actually sounded quite…good.

113

I wasn't about to say so out loud, of course, but that made a change. Ozzy hadn't made a really good solo album for several years, not since his first two, in fact, a decade before. Maybe the nineties would see another upsurge in his popularity. Not that he wasn't still big; his shows still sold out in America, that was for sure. And all his albums, whatever their individual merits, had gone platinum. Outside America, though, a string of so-so releases had seen his popularity plateau, as they say in the biz. That is, they went in high in the charts – and straight out again, his fanbase always remaining strong but never actually growing, just rejuvenating as each new generation of 15-year-old boys came along and discovered Black Sabbath – and those two groundbreaking Ozzy solo albums – for themselves, the same way my generation had 'discovered' artists before our time like Hendrix, the Stones and The Beatles. Anyway, what did it really matter? As Sharon had told me many times, if all else failed there was always the Black Sabbath reunion, though of course Ozzy always shat on the very idea. 'No way!' he'd declare. 'I'm not going near those cunts again!' But I'd have bet anything on it happening sooner or later. There was just too much money waiting to be made for Sharon not to consider it seriously one day, surely?

Finally, the tape stopped and the air was filled at last with silence. Well, not silence but enough room to speak. It was then I produced what I hoped Ozzy would consider a nice little present. Even when Ozzy was on the wagon he had a fondness for the odd smoke of marijuana. This being LA, a small gift of some fine weed was also considered polite, in the way of a house guest bringing a nice bottle of wine with them. So I had brought with me a small polythene wrap of pot. Nothing roof-lifting, just enough for a couple of smokes before dinner, to sharpen the appetite.

'Put it away mate,' he said, eyeing the discreet green bundle with what looked like pity. Oh, dear, I thought, a false move. I hadn't realised his latest wagon-riding precluded a bit of dope. Then he leaned over and reached for something behind the couch. A large black bin liner. 'Here,' he said, 'try this instead.'

I opened up the large plastic bag and looked inside. Oh my god! It was full of marijuana; enough to keep a large community of unreconstructed hippies going for about a month, by the looks of it.

'What's this?' I asked unnecessarily.

'What do you fucking think?'

'Um...did you want me to roll one then?'

'Naw, fuck that. Use this instead,' he said, pulling out another surprise from behind the couch. It was large blue bong.

'Look at that beauty,' he said. 'What do you think of that?'

Well, it was certainly big. And blue. And brand new, apparently. 'I bought it from some head shop down on Melrose this morning,' he told me. 'It's top of the range,' he added proudly.

We stoked her up. Three or four hits later, I was coughing my guts up and struggling to keep both eyes pointing in the same direction. This went far beyond a little chuff before dinner. This was a lethal weapon. I sat there coughing and spluttering as Ozzy sat next to me laughing. Why wasn't he coughing violently too? The trick, he said, was to take little sips of brandy in-between. 'Helps cool down the lungs,' he explained. I had a few sips but the brandy only made my head start spinning even faster. Oh dear, oh dear, oh dear...

'Hang on,' he said. 'I know what will clear your head out.' Not from behind the couch this time but tucked behind an ornament on a shelf on the wall. Another polythene bag, not nearly half as big and filled with something white, not green. 'This'll fucking sort us out!' he guffawed as he went to fetch a mirror and a blade.

And that was how we spent the next four or five hours, chundering over the bong, followed by 'little sips' of brandy and a couple more snorts of coke. Not that I was complaining. That wouldn't begin until I woke up the next day with what Ozzy described not inaccurately as 'a head like a cunt full of shit.' Indeed, an evening of weed, wine and coke was a fairly typical night in for most people living in West Hollywood back then. The main difference was the sheer enthusiasm Ozzy brought to the proceedings. Just like the way he had consumed so many bottles of wine that time a few years before when he'd cooked me Sunday lunch, there were never any half-measures in Ozzy's drugging. It was all or nothing, a sign perhaps of his addictive nature. Or perhaps it was just the way they had done things in his day, back in the late sixties and early seventies when they were writing the rulebook on this stuff.

At about one in the morning, he asked Tony his driver to take us for a spin down Sunset Boulevard, just for something to do. We stopped off at an all-night store called the Pink Dot that sold anything and everything you could possibly want in the middle of night, from booze and cigarettes to the big fancy chocolate cake that caught Ozzy's attention. They put it in a big white box for us tied with ribbons but when we got it back to his apartment neither of us could actually eat it, so we just sat there, sticking our fingers in it then sucking the icing off them. Earlier in the evening I had remarked that I liked his trousers – loose-fitting abstract-patterned beach trousers popular in LA at the time called Crazy Pants. Now he went to his bedroom and retrieved an unwrapped pair – he had bought '10 or 12 pairs,' he said – and gave them to me, and I got up and put them straight on and as he loaded up the bong again.

'Here, I've just remembered,' he said. 'I've got something that'll make you piss yourself. It's a video Steve Vai gave me...'

Steve Vai was the current hotshot guitarist in LA. A child protégé who had got his break as a teenager playing for Frank Zappa, followed by starring roles with a succession of bigger and more successful rock acts – David Lee Roth, Whitesnake – where his vampirish good looks and almost supernatural ability on the guitar had turned him into a superstar in America. Now he was a solo star in his own right and the fans – particularly the female fans – battled for his attention. Ozzy put the video on and there was a woman slowly doing a striptease while talking to the camera. 'You see, Steve, when I see you on stage, it just makes me want to act crazy...'

When she was completely naked she began doing odd things with her vagina: rubbing it vigorously as though trying to remove a stain, then inserting various household objects up there – lit candles, long brown fingers of candy, all sorts of weird and not quite wonderful things.

'Are you watching Steve?' she breathed heavily.

Ozzy could hardly contain himself. 'No, but *I am*, darling!' he roared with laughter.

She continued with her act. It was certainly an attention grabber. 'Oh, Steve, oh Steve,' she groaned, 'I can almost feel you inside me...'

The woman wasn't unattractive but what she was doing was so gross it went beyond porn, into a whole new realm of degradation. I didn't know what you'd call it. Not the nudity, just the *concept*. Next thing, her vagina started making little farting noises. 'Watch this, Steve,' she smiled, and she crouched over a lit candle, made a little pussy fart and blew the thing out. 'Am I a clever girl, Steve?'

'Ten out of ten, darling!' laughed Ozzy. 'You should be on *The Twilight Zone*...'

We sat there laughing together. What else could you do, the world was full of freaks? But the longer the tape kept playing the less funny the whole spectacle became. Soon the laughter petered out and the mood turned distinctly maudlin. Just then, Tony – who was sharing the apartment with Ozzy – came in to say he was going to bed and to remind him he had to be up early the next morning to start work again in the studio. That brought Ozzy's mood right down. And that's when it started – the moaning and groaning about how hard he had it.

'I mean, I fucking love my wife,' he was saying, 'but being married to your manager, I mean, it ain't no fucking picnic, old bean.'

'No,' I sympathised, 'I expect not.'

It went on and on – and on. I tuned out for most of it, as I always did. I knew where this was all going and for me that meant calling a cab as quickly as possible and going home to bed and, when I woke, cunt full of shit time.

Then suddenly, he jumped up and cried: 'You're right!' What was I right about? 'I'm gonna phone her now and tell her.' Phone who and tell them what?

He stumbled over to the phone and began dialling as I sat there staring at him, wondering what was going on.

'Sharon?' I heard him wail down the phone. 'I'm sat here with Mick Wall and we've been talking and Mick agrees with me, I fucking love you as my wife but I don't want to be married to my manager any more.'

Oh, shit! I couldn't believe my ears! What the fuck was he doing?

He sat on the phone for a few more minutes, but by now it was clear it was Sharon doing most of the talking, Ozzy just nodding his head muttering along. 'Yeah…yeah…yeah, well, you know… yeah…yeah…no…'

When he eventually hung up, I asked him: what did she say? 'She says she wants a divorce,' he said dolefully.

Oh, fuck…

'Phone her back quick,' I said, 'and tell her you've changed your mind. And for fuck's sake tell her it's got nothing to do with me!'

'No,' he said, weepily. 'It's too late now, she's all pissed off.'

Great, that was all I needed. Sharon pissed off at me, too.

I looked over at him. 'Man, I gotta go,' I said. 'I'm fried…'

'I'll call you a cab,' he said.

We sat there in silence waiting for the cab to come. When it did, finally, and the buzzer went, I left Ozzy still sitting on the couch and staggered down the corridor to the elevator. As the doors opened, I could hear the music begin to blare from his apartment again, his voice, now sounding somewhat cracked, yelling over the top. How did the neighbours put up with it, I wondered? And what would Sharon say the next time I saw her? I imagined her giving me the 'dirty motherfucker' treatment and winced.

Shit, shit, shit, shit, shit…

Act II
Scene Two:

When the World Comes Crashing Down

Many years later, so long after the event that it hardly mattered any more, Don Arden was still banging on about the fact that it was he – not his daughter, Sharon – that had made Ozzy Osbourne the star he became after being unceremoniously bundled out of Black Sabbath. Sitting with Don in his Park Lane apartment throughout the summer of 2002, working through his scattered memories for his official biography, there were so many genuinely visionary moments from his career to talk about – his pioneering decision to bring the original generation of American rock'n'roll stars to Britain and Europe in the 1950s; the way he transformed the Star Club in Germany from a cheap Hamburg shit-hole into one of the most influential and name-checked venues in popular music history; his discovery of one of the defining groups of Swinging Sixties London, the Small Faces; his manoeuvring in the early seventies of The Move into both the Electric Light Orchestra and Wizzard…the list was huge and impressive. And yet time and again he returned to an old familiar theme.

'People go on now about how Sharon turned Ozzy into a star,' he grumbled, 'Absolute rubbish! I was his manager! I was the one who took him into my house, gave him somewhere to clean himself up and sort himself out, she was just the day-to-day run-around for him. By the time he started again he was on five thousand dollars a night. By the end of it he was making a hundred grand a night. Who did that for him? My daughter? Don't make me laugh. Oh, she did a good job in the years after that, I'll grant you that. But people forget he was already a star by then. And who made him that way? Me, that's who! Me!'

He even claimed it was he – and not Sharon – who was responsible for the career-defining moment when Ozzy bit the head off a dove at the CBS Records convention in 1981. 'I was the one pulling out all the stops, trying to get everyone in America interested in him – not Sharon! It was me that organised the get-together with the heads of all the various departments at CBS in Los Angeles. It was even me that wrote the little speech for him to give, some old bollocks about how he did it all for love, not money. It was at the end of that he was supposed to pull out the doves and release them into the air. I thought everybody would go, 'Coo! How wonderful!' Except he'd polished off a bottle of brandy in the car on the way over there and went mad.' He shook his head. 'And who turned it round when it all went wrong? No, not Sharon! Me! Everyone else just did what they were told – including my daughter.'

I wasn't about to argue with the old man. Even in his seventies, he was still quite a formidable character. With the Alzheimer's starting to eat away at his brain he was no longer as mentally lithe as when I had first met him just a few months before, but he was still physically tenacious, and even if he wasn't up to it, he was certainly able to pick up a phone and summon some old crony who was. Nevertheless, I couldn't help but wonder where he was at. I knew Sharon was equally capable of rewriting history too when it suited her. But there seemed little doubt that it was Sharon – not Don – who had summoned all the king's men when it came to putting Humpty Dumpty back together again. Not only that, but having got him back sitting high on the wall, somehow managed to keep him there for the next quarter-century.

All that said, however, there is equally no doubt that both Sharon and Don – and Ozzy – all benefited very early on from a huge stroke of luck that none of them could have helped manufacture on their own. And that was the discovery of the person who would actually write Ozzy a whole new soundtrack to live his life by, and build the foundations of a proper solo career. Not one built just on crazy antics or a controversial reputation – the very things, in fact, which had gotten him thrown out of Sabbath in the first place – but on actual old-fashioned concepts like making good music, groundbreaking albums and killer live shows. That person's name was Randy Rhoads.

Twenty-two-year-old Rhoads was the quiet, Californian-born, classically trained guitarist who would hand Ozzy the musical platform upon which his reputation as a solo artist still rests today. Indeed, nearly 30 years on, his live set still relies heavily on those first two, Rhoads-scored albums: *Blizzard of Ozz* (1980) and *Diary of a Madman* (1981), and the handful of classic songs that would define Ozzy Osbourne as a recording artist in his own right, out from the formidable shadow of Black Sabbath: 'Crazy Train', 'Mr. Crowley', 'I Don't Know', 'Suicide Solution', 'Flying High Again', and the anthemic title track of his second album, 'Diary Of A Madman'.

Born in Santa Monica in 1956, the youngest of three children, Randy was a year old when his father, William, split up with his mother, Delores, though he apparently stayed in touch with his youngest son. Delores had run the Musonia School of Music in North Hollywood, since 1949, and all her children were musical. Randy was seven when he began tinkering with his grandfather's old Gibson 'Army-Navy' acoustic guitar. As fascinated by rock as any other kid growing up in California in the sixties, he also gravitated towards both classical and folk forms on the guitar. By the time he formed his first semi-pro band, Violet Fox (after his mother's middle name, Violet) he was already regarded locally as a guitar protégé.

When he was 14, and with his older brother Kelle on drums, Violet Fox performed regularly in the 'Grand Salon' of Musonia. By the time he was 17 he was the guitarist in LA band Quiet Riot, fronted by vocalist Kevin DuBrow, who started out in well-known Sunset Strip clubs the Whisky a Go Go and the Starwood and soon landed a deal with the Japanese end of CBS Records, where their first two albums were minor hits. Though they would later score massive hits in the US with their cover of Slade's 'Cumon Feel The Noize' and 'Mama Weer All Crazee Now', at the time Randy auditioned for Ozzy's new solo outfit, Quiet Riot were in the doldrums and he had began teaching guitar part-time at his mother's school.

Ozzy and Sharon had already sat through weeks of auditions at rehearsal studios in LA before Randy walked in late one night. 'It was about two o'clock in the morning,' Sharon told me, 'and when he walked in we all thought he was girl, he was so blonde and tiny and good-looking.' In fact, Ozzy didn't think anything at all at first as he was curled up asleep on a couch in the corner of the room. When Sharon shook him awake, in his dazed state he couldn't understand what some blonde chick was doing holding a Gibson strapped to her thigh, and an expression on her face so calm, then so murderous as she started hitting those chords.

'It was a guy called Dana Strum [bassist of mid-eighties power-balladeers Slaughter] who turned me on to Randy,' Ozzy would later tell me. 'He brought him to the studio one night. I was absolutely arseholed, lying across the studio desk. Randy was so pretty I thought he must be gay. He says, "Whaddaya want me to play?" I says, "You got a solo?" He says, "Well, kinda…" He had a tiny fucking amp but he played and I just went…*what!?!* I remember thinking, in my haze, this is not really happening, it can't be. Cos this guy…you hadn't heard stuff like that before. Kind of like Eddie Van Halen, who was the new kid on the block then, but about a thousand times better!'

Randy wasn't only an innovative guitarist whose more hyper style would redefine the sound of hard rock in the eighties, he was to become the new jewel in Ozzy's crown, writing the music for all the songs. He was also, as Sharon says, 'An unbelievably sweet kid who wouldn't say boo to a goose. We both loved him.' Kind-hearted, softly spoken, Randy would often be the go-between, in fact, whenever Ozzy and Sharon started rowing, which they always did from day one. 'We were like our own little family,' said Sharon. Recognising both Randy's talent and his uncanny ability to fit in with her and Ozzy's increasingly mad world, she immediately signed him up for management too. Something she would make a point of not doing with the rest of the initial recruits of Ozzy's band: journeyman bassist Bob Daisley and former Uriah Heep drummer Lee Kerslake – both hired during a return trip home to England for Ozzy, and very much not Sharon's choices for the jobs.

'I never would have had Lee Kerslake, or Bob Daisley in the band, if I'd been there, taking care of things right at the very end of those auditions,' she told me in no uncertain terms. 'But Ozzy went ahead and recruited Lee into his band, and when he arrived back in London for a couple of weeks, he bumped into Bob Daisley somewhere along the line and invited him then and there to join the band.' She rolled her eyes. Daisley had been a member of one of Don's old bands, Widowmaker, and before that Mungo Jerry. 'Bob had rung me up about the gig a few months before,' said Sharon. 'I tried to make the gig sound terrible, because I didn't want to have to tell him we didn't want him. He'll hate me for saying this, but it's true. So I said, "Well, it's basically a side-man situation and not what you're looking for, Bob". Then the next thing I know, they're starting to rehearse for the first album and Bob Daisley is the bass player!' As for Lee Kerslake, she said, 'I knew absolutely nothing about him except that he was supposed to be a good drummer. When I first clapped eyes on him though, I thought he looked like an old man. I thought, "Great, here we are trying to get Ozzy off the ground with a whole new generation of rock fans, and here we've got this amazing blonde kid on guitar, and now I've got these two old duffers as well! Good work Ozzy – not!"'

What Sharon wasn't so quick to admit, however, was that Daisley had more going for him than just his bass playing. He was also a more than capable lyricist, as his work on several Ozzy albums over the years – including his first two breakthrough releases – has demonstrated. In Sabbath, Ozzy had rarely written anything, not in the conventional sense, anyway, of putting actual words down on a piece of paper. Though Ozzy might sing a melody line, the lyrics had almost all come from Geezer Butler. Working to a similar brief as a solo artist, I once watched Ozzy and Bob working on a lyric together in the studio. Ozzy would caterwaul a line or two, Bob would scribble something down at his music stand, then read the lines back to Ozzy, who might say something like, 'Yeah, great.' Or: 'Naw, I don't wanna sing about devils on this one. Can't you make it more, like, about a girl?' And Bob would go, 'Yeah, sure,' and start scribbling again, before reading out the corrections, to which Ozzy would again either go, 'Yeah, great,' or possibly grimace and go off for a cigarette, leaving Bob to get on with it.

All of which is as legitimate a way to write material as any other, as is the practice of omitting any reference to the songwriting input of certain individuals, as long as everyone agrees to the arrangement upfront – fairly standard music business practice, going back to Elvis and beyond and right the way up to Madonna. The logic being: *you* might have written the song but if *I* record it, it will sell 10 times more – or possibly several million times more – than it would if you the songwriter recorded it. In return the songwriter might receive a straightforward flat fee or a royalty rate. In Daisley's case, whatever he felt he had agreed with Sharon, it was never enough and both he and Kerslake successfully sued Ozzy in 1986 to have their songwriting and performance credits reinstated on the first two albums after Sharon had deliberately omitted them. They also claimed alleged unpaid royalties, even giving bitter interviews to music magazines complaining of being unfairly treated. Even though Bob would routinely return to the fold, rejoining the band for the 1983 world tour and contributing lyrics to the next four Ozzy studio albums (whether credited or not), he and Kerslake renewed their litigation in 2002 when they once again sued for unpaid royalties. Sharon's shrewd response: to delete the original recordings and reissue new versions with the bass and drum tracks re-recorded by other musicians.

Meanwhile, back in 1980, the star of the show was undoubtedly Randy. Bob might have written the greatest lyrics in the world but they would all have come to nought had it not been for the extraordinary music Randy was now putting them to. 'I remember going in there to record "Crazy Train" – vaguely,' Ozzy told me. 'You've got to remember I was drinking a hell of a lot and getting wrecked out of my mind all the time in those days. But I remember going there thinking, "Well, no one gives a fuck about me any more anyway, so I'm just going to go in there and make a record the best way I can, in a way that will make me love it, fuck everyone else." And Randy Rhoads was just nothing but a star the whole time. Randy was a fucking darling, he would spend forever working on the music. It was like a golden ray of sunshine working with him. That was when I started to think there might be more to life than just bitter memories of Black Sabbath.'

By the time Ozzy had begun his first solo tour of the US, there was no doubt about it: Ozzy had a new playmate on stage; someone who not only took up the slack musically, filling the gaping hole left by Black Sabbath no longer being the band Ozzy sang with, but who actually made Ozzy feel good about himself. Tony Iommi had always treated Ozzy as a joke, someone to put up with. Randy, who had been teaching kids Sabbath songs on the guitar before he met Ozzy, treated him with respect and devotion, even love.

Sharon, meanwhile, was having to fill the gaping hole left by her father, who was far too busy running his record company and swanning around the world with the mega-successful ELO to schlep around on a tour bus with Ozzy. Fortunately for Ozzy, Sharon was more than just a chip off the old block. Proving it by facing down promoters who liked to try their luck by underpaying the band, or recalcitrant record company drones, men used to giving artists the old soft-soap treatment instead of going out and doing their jobs. Once, at an in-store signing, she leapt on a photographer she recognised as a bootlegger – the kind who would take shots of an artist then sell prints outside their shows, making several thousand dollars in the process – and proceeded to punch his lights out. Not bad for a five foot nothing woman. Even more impressive, she tackled one promoter who tried to charge her for $6,000 worth of pre-concert advertising by head-butting him and kicking him in the balls. As she later recalled, 'Apart from my father, I had no role model, so to a certain extent I had to make up the rules as I went along.' Word spread quickly throughout the biz: you didn't tell Sharon Arden what to do. Or else.

When Sharon and Ozzy then became an item, it made them both even more determined not to be pushed around – even by her father, who viewed their affair with utter disdain, despite the huge and sudden success they were now enjoying, and which he would insist on taking all the credit for as the years rolled by. As Ozzy's manager, not to mention record company boss – a clear conflict of interest for any other artist, just another neat contractual tie up to Don – all monies now being made went straight into Don's various accounts. Despite the success Sharon and Ozzy were now enjoying, they were, as she put it to me, 'living hand to mouth on the fucking tour bus. We didn't have a pot to shit in.' A situation Sharon knew she would have to deal with sooner or later, but for now remained too in fear of her all-powerful father to tackle.

At least the band was now functioning fully. Having dispensed with the services of the grizzly Kerslake and Daisley – replacing them with the more youthful-looking Americans, drummer Tommy Aldridge and bassist Rudy Sarzo – Sharon contented herself at least with the fact that Ozzy's music would only get better and better. And then, suddenly, even that thought was taken away from them.

For Ozzy Osbourne, the day the music died wasn't when he was thrown out of Black Sabbath, betrayed by the band he had done as much as anyone to make world famous. It came three years later, after he'd achieved what he'd previously thought impossible and come back from rock bottom to find success as a solo artist. When the young man who had done more even than Sharon or Don, or even Ozzy, to help put his career back on a firm musical footing – Randy Rhoads – died in one of the most dreadful, unnecessary and just plain tragic accidents in the annals of rock'n'roll.

It was 19 March 1982, and Ozzy and Sharon were on the tour bus with the rest of the band on their way from Knoxville, Tennessee, where they had performed another sold-out show just a few hours before, to Orlando, Florida, where an open-air festival date later that day awaited with Foreigner, then one of the most successful American rock bands in the world. Sharon was asleep in her and Ozzy's own private lounge at the back of the bus, most of the band sleeping in their own section. The only people awake, apart from the bus driver, Andrew Aycock, and – though Sharon didn't know it at the time – his ex-wife, who was sitting upfront with him, were Ozzy and Randy – whiling away the small hours having the sort of intimate 'what if?' conversation the wee small hours are wont to encourage in anyone not yet adrift in slumberland – and Rachel Youngblood, a middle-aged black woman who worked as a make-up and costume dresser on the tour and who had been part of Sharon's home life for so many years she was regarded as one of the family.

Aycock's depot happened to be on the route for Orlando, and with the bus's air conditioning system failing intermittently, he decided to pick up a new one. Woken by the bus pulling over and the driver's door opening, tour manager Jake Duncan and band keyboardist Don Airey decided to stretch their legs too. Three years later, Sharon would tell me what happened while still fighting back the tears. 'As coincidence would have it, the bus driver's ex-wife had turned up at the gig the night before and had ended up travelling with us to Florida on the bus. I didn't want her on the bus, it was jammed tight with people anyway, but all the same she ended up coming along with the driver for the overnight ride. The driver and his ex-wife hadn't had a happy divorce, they weren't on friendly terms. So they were both up all night talking. He was on coke, when they did the autopsy on the bus driver's body he was full of coke. He was up all night driving this fucking big bus, he was yabbering away endlessly to a woman he didn't like, and by eight o'clock in the morning the bus, with all of us still asleep on it, arrived in his depot.'

The out-of-the-way spot Aycock had brought them all to was actually the homestead of the bus company's owner, Jerry Calhoun: part bus depot, part landing strip for small light aircraft, situated on a large plot of land in Leesburg, Florida, with three buildings arranged around a large empty field, including Calhoun's own mansion home. The addled driver had once been a professional pilot before his licence was revoked after he was held responsible for the death of a small boy in a helicopter accident years before. 'Of course, we didn't know any of this at the time,' Sharon pointed out. 'All that only came out after Randy's death. Anyway, this fool took our tour manager at that time, Jake, and Don Airey up in this little plane. Don wanted to take pictures of the bus and the driver starts showing off a bit while they were all up there, doing stupid whirligigs and all that nonsense, just so Don could take his pictures.'

When the plane touched down, Aycock extended the same invitation to the only other people still awake on the bus: Randy and Rachel. 'The stupid thing is that Randy and Rachel both hated flying, absolutely loathed it,' said Sharon, shaking her head. 'Now Rachel worked for me, but she was also a dear old friend of mine. She was 56 years old, and she was the band's dresser on the road, and she also took care of my clothes on the road. A lovely, lovely lady and she'd had a bad heart all her life. We'd go to Disneyland together in California, and Rachel would come with us, but she'd never take a ride, never! And Randy, you couldn't bribe him onto a joyride on a plane, usually. Earlier in the tour we'd had five days' break in the schedule and everybody flew to Los Angeles for some rest, but not Randy. He wanted to hang around, drive down to the beach and hang out because he didn't want to take a plane.' There had been a 'terrible plane crash in Washington that winter [that] had scared the hell out of Randy, and he simply refused to fly unless the band needed him to.'

She gulped some tea and continued. 'Anyway, they all start telling Randy and Rachel it's fun, it's fun, and in the end persuaded them to go up in the plane for a ride. Randy and Rachel eventually go up in the plane and what Ozzy and I are convinced happened is this: this stupid ex-pilot cowboy took them up in the plane, and his ex-wife was stood by the bus. She'd got off the bus and was standing there watching the plane fly around. And we think that for one split second the pilot said "fuck you", and went for it. He flew straight at the bus, his wing ploughed into the top of the bus, and from there went into one of the houses behind where the bus was parked, then it exploded in the garage of the house...' She stopped, her voice faltering as her mind relived the awful scene.

Everyone on the plane – the bus driver, Randy and Rachel – was killed in the crash. Fortunately, despite slicing a hole in the bus no one else was hurt. Not physically anyway. The mental scars though are something both Ozzy and Sharon are still dealing with today: Ozzy because he had lost both the closest collaborator of his musical life and a good friend; Sharon because she had lost someone she admired and respected as an artist and very much loved as a person. So much so, in fact, that, years later, she would admit she had once slept with him. It had been late at night, she said, on the tour bus while Ozzy and everyone else had been sleeping, but it had not been the start of an affair, she insisted, more the act of a touching union between two very, very close friends. Speaking more than a quarter of a century later, she even suggested that Ozzy had known about her and Randy's one-off secret tryst and had taken it for what it was. 'Ozzy knows and has never wanted to discuss it,' she recalled. 'But don't read any dissatisfaction into it. Ozzy knows the one-time occurrence was loving, not lustful.'

Now Randy was gone – forever. Later, when press reports claimed the plane had merely been 'buzzing' the bus, Sharon was even more upset. 'All the press stories started saying that they were all messing around in the plane, but Randy and Rachel weren't like that when it came to flying, they hated it!' she told me. 'If it had been Don Airey I would have said, "Yes, all right, absolutely, he was messing around", because Don's just a big kid. But Randy hated flying, and Rachel…a 56-year-old woman? So we think that he looked down from the sky, this fucking pilot, saw his ex-wife who he hated, and said "fuck you!" And he was on coke. He was out of his mind…'

As Sharon had been asleep on the bus at the time the plane hit it, the truth is neither she nor anyone else will ever really know why the accident occurred. Yet it was something she felt strongly enough about to repeat in her own book, 20 years later when she wrote: 'The autopsy showed that his [the bus driver's] body was full of cocaine, and I heard later that he'd already killed someone in a helicopter crash, yet he walked free.'

For the record, an autopsy revealed that Aycock had a trace of cocaine in his system at the time of the crash, while Randy's toxicology report revealed no illicit drugs. The investigation by the NTSB (the official American body that investigates accidental air deaths) also determined that Aycock's medical certificate had expired and that his biennial flight review required of all pilots was overdue. In other words, he shouldn't have been allowed anywhere near an aeroplane, let alone a tour bus.

Randy's funeral was held a fortnight later at the First Lutheran Church in Burbank, California, where he had been a regular part of the congregation as a child. He was later interred at Mountain View Cemetery in San Bernardino, California, where his grandparents are also buried. When we spoke about it not long after, Ozzy said: 'Randy's death was a horrendous ordeal for everybody involved, because we were all there and we all saw it happen, and we saw what happened afterwards. It was just the most terrible thing. It's like something you see in movies but could never ever visualise happening to you. But there's two people that you love in bits on the ground and you think: "What the fuck's going on?" I think me and Sharon lay in bed at night shaking for about two weeks afterwards…'

An untimely, unfair death, the date is remembered every year at his graveside by gifts of flowers from an assembly of fans in California. Ozzy and Sharon still send their own bouquet of flowers every year as well, and Randy is remembered with a mixture of adulation and mystery by the fans, and with nothing but love by Ozzy and Sharon. 'After all the heartbreak of Randy's death, I just felt I couldn't face it any more,' Ozzy later confessed. 'I told Sharon, "It's all over, I'm finished". We'd all worked so hard for so long, and the madness that was already going down on that tour had been getting to me, and then Randy got killed. That final thing was just too much for me.' He shook his head sorrowfully.

Having fought Black Sabbath, her father and his record company, miscreant promoters and unscrupulous merchandisers, Sharon, however, was determined not to let even this setback prevent Ozzy from maintaining the career path she had so expertly steered him down so far. Knowing it was now or never, she insisted he find a replacement guitarist for the band within a fortnight of Randy's death, somebody temporary if need be. The thing was just to get someone, and as for Ozzy's retirement plans, she told him, 'You'd better not say anything like that to me again, Johnny Osbourne. Now get out on that stage and do your job!'

'I look back on that time now,' Ozzy would tell me, 'and I know in my heart that if we hadn't carried on as soon as we did, if we'd taken all the time we eventually did take to find a real replacement for Randy, I would never have climbed back on stage again. None of us would have. So we just took the first bloke that came along.'

Who happened to be a young gun-for-hire from London named Bernie Torme. Given only 10 days to try and fill Randy's shoes, Torme lasted just three weeks before throwing in the towel, simply unable to deal with the situation. 'Bernie couldn't take the pressure, simple as that,' Sharon shrugged. 'He couldn't take the pressure we were all under at the time. It was too much for him, he hated it.' By now grieving fans were turning up at Ozzy's shows carrying huge hand-lettered signs bearing the now immortal name of Randy Rhoads. Every day Bernie seemed to walk in on someone else crying, not least Ozzy and Sharon, who were 'like zombies.' And while Ozzy was going to pieces backstage, the fans out front were acting even more hysterically than usual, screaming and crying, some even acting with hostility towards the new guitarist brought to replace who was for them – and Ozzy and Sharon it seemed – simply irreplaceable. 'Poor cunt couldn't wait to get away,' said Ozzy. 'And I can't say I blame him, I felt like running off somewhere far away many times myself on that tour. But Bernie didn't leave us in the shit. In those three weeks we had Brad Gillis rehearsed and ready to take over properly, at least on this one tour.'

Gillis was an older, more experienced guitarist from San Francisco then busy getting his own band together called Night Ranger, who agreed to help out until the end of the tour. And so yet another seemingly insurmountable tragedy once again became just one more building block in the myth of Ozzy Osbourne. Twenty-five years later, however, Ozzy would confess to me that even if Randy had lived he doesn't think he would have stayed in the band for too much longer anyway. I was taken aback. But why not?

'Because I don't think he'd be playing rock'n'roll at all any more. He was writing his own thing, his own musical language. His mother was a music teacher and she couldn't work it out, but he was up night after night writing this stuff down. Then on that last tour, one night he says to me, "You know what, I think I'm gonna quit rock'n'roll". I said, "Why? We're just breaking it big time, what's up with you?" He says, "I've tasted it. But I want to get a degree in classical music". I said, "Are you out of your fucking mind? Another few albums and you'll be able to buy a university!" Then the next [thing] was he died and that was it, as far as I was concerned I was finished, that was the end of me too. It was Sharon that dragged me off my pity pot – again. And she was right. I mean, what else are you supposed to do? Become a fucking monk? By then, my whole life was out of control anyway. I lost my father in '77. Then Sabbath fired me. Then Sharon entered my life and I found Randy. Then Randy died…So many times, I thought it was fucking over.'

So many times, it would have been – if not for Sharon.

Act II
Scene Three:

A Marriage Made in Hell

Sitting with Ozzy in a suite at the Dorchester hotel in London in the summer of 2005, both of us sipping tea, he asks me: 'Do you still smoke wonga?'

I shake my head. 'Not for years.'

He shakes his head. 'Naw, me neither. I just can't handle it any more, I'm too fucking old, mate.'

We both take another sip of tea. 'Coke?' he asks.

'Fuck off! Why, you got any?'

He laughs: 'I'd run a mile now if someone brought some out.'

'I know what you mean.'

'Cigarettes?' he tries again.

I shake my head again. 'Doctors won't let me.'

He scratches his hair. 'Fucking doctors, they ruin everything, don't they?'

I nod. He looks at me dolefully. 'I don't know about you, but I've gone completely the other way now. They say an ex-smoker is worse than a non-smoker and it's true. I can't stand to be around it. Luckily,

137

in California you can't even smoke in a fucking chimney now. But I was in a restaurant here the other night with Sharon, and there was this woman at the adjacent table smoking one after another right through her meal. Then I look again and she's got a fucking cigar in her trap! Sharon goes, "She probably goes to bed with a fucking pipe up her cunt!"'

I burst out laughing. That's the thing with Ozzy. It was never the drugs or the drink or even the rock'n'roll that made him such good company. It was because he was genuine – genuinely funny; genuinely interesting; genuinely a good bloke who got up to lots of bad things. You get the feeling talking to him as an older man that there isn't anything he did as a younger man he wouldn't do again under similar circumstances. The drink and the drugs and even the rock'n'roll were just adjuncts; backdrops, wallpaper, hairclips…not much of anything at all, even though they did nearly kill him at one time, or land him in some pretty strange places.

Like the time when he and Sharon were living on the road together, travelling America in the tour bus with Randy and Rachel and the rest of the guys, and they arrived in Texas – pissed. It was only a couple of months before the plane crash in 1982 but things were already getting weird, Ozzy and Sharon both drinking in those days, both fighting each other. 'Either fighting each other or fucking,' as he later put it.

'It was always a very passionate relationship, wasn't it?' I remark.

'Are you taking the fucking piss?' he says. 'Some of the worst fights I've ever had in my life have been with Sharon. Especially in the early days, there'd be blood all over the walls – my blood! She's much worse than any bloke.'

So there they were in Texas, in San Antonio – a small desert town split between a heavy but discreet Mafia presence (very little petty crime in Old San Atone) and the kind of longhorn cowboys that make John Wayne in his prime look like a girl – and Ozzy has been so out of control Sharon decides the only way to stop him going out and getting himself shot is to literally steal all his clothes. So what does he do? He finds one of her dresses and puts it on. Then goes out and gets drunk. In San Antonio, probably the US murder capital for homosexuals and transvestites.

According to Ozzy, it was actually for a photo-shoot for the British music paper, *Melody Maker*. 'They wanted to do a shot of me in front of The Alamo,' he explained, 'and I had drunk a bottle and a half of cognac before everything was ready for us to go over there and do the business. So I'm totally out of my head already, right? Anyway, just for a laugh I dressed up in some [of Sharon's] clothing. I thought it would be a good laugh for the pictures, and I was so drunk I couldn't think of anything else anyway. And that was my big downfall; I was as drunk as a skunk, and when you're drunk like that you tend to piss a lot. The pictures were taking a while so I stopped to take a leak. I spotted this bit of old tumbled down brick wall, and I thought that would do…'

Unfortunately, that 'old, tumbled down brick wall' was part of The Alamo itself. It's important to bear in mind, at this point, that The Alamo is a national shrine in America; an iconic monument to the American Dream writ large; a shrine for the brave cavalry soldiers who gave their lives in the fight for Texan independence from the Mexicans, as personified by General Santa Anna. Or put another way, whatever you do in San Antonio, you don't piss on The Alamo. Not unless you want to get yourself shot in the head – or at the very least arrested.

'I'm pissing away quite happily on this old brick wall,' said Ozzy, 'when this old guy comes running up to me and starts going fucking crazy. He's screaming. "You dirty bastard, you filthy motherfucker, you son of a bitch, you filthy faggot! Ain't cha got no respect? You're relieving yourself on a public shrine!" I wondered what the hell was going on, you know. The old guy is ranting and raving away about national shrines and pissing, screaming and waving his hands in the air, and I'm standing there in my dress trying to calm the poor bugger down. It was unbelievable. Then two enormous cops arrive on the scene in a meat-wagon and the old geezer starts screaming again: "Here he is, the dirty bastard! He's the one that pissed on The Alamo!" Drunk and out of control though I was, I said to myself, "Fuck me, I've pissed on The Alamo. Now I'm in trouble." How the fuck do you talk your way out of that, you know?'

Questioned by the disbelieving cops Ozzy admitted it was true and that, yes, he had in fact urinated on one of America's most treasured national monuments, adding: 'But it was a genuine mistake and anyway, when the Mexicans were attacking it there must have been more than just piss running down the walls.' Maybe so but it was not an argument likely to endear him to the local gun-toting constabulary. Ozzy was arrested and thrown into the back of the police van, his make-up running down his nose, his dress a shambles. Ozzy was driven to the station and locked in a cell. Waiting for him in there was another prisoner, a mean-looking red-eyed monster who announced he'd been arrested for murdering his wife. 'Apparently,' said Ozzy, 'He was supposed to have beaten her to death, or something. I nearly shit myself. What a bizarre situation. Anyway, he asked me who I was and I told him and he said, "Bullshit". And then he had a think and he stood up and screamed: "You *are* Ozzy

Osbourne!" Then he started screaming at me to go and see the Governor on his behalf. He kept yelling, "You can get me out of this! You can do it if anyone can! They'll believe you!" At which point I knew for certain I was locked away with a complete lunatic.'

Informed of his latest misadventure, back at the hotel Sharon was so furious she was tempted to 'let him fucking rot.' Then, realising that she was his only hope – as usual – she roused herself and got busy on the phone, trying to get a lawyer down to the cop station to sort out this latest mess. Some hours later, a by now sober and very sorry-looking Ozzy was brought before a disbelieving local court judge who fined him and, worse, banned him from ever performing in San Antonio again.

The concerts themselves were also increasingly riotous affairs. Back on tour in the wake of Randy's death, it was a toss up over who was behaving worse: Ozzy or his fans. Madness seemed to breed more madness as word spread. No longer content with merely throwing offal, kids had started throwing bottles and fireworks around at gigs. At one, Sharon had to be taken to hospital after a Cherry Bomb exploded at her feet. 'It blew up right in front of my eyes and it threw a chunk of the stage floor into the side of my neck,' she told me. 'I had to be run to the local hospital to have this piece of the floor removed from my neck. I was probably blinded completely for about five minutes, and the explosion turned me deaf for a time too.'

Ozzy dealt with it all the same way he had all his other problems: he began hitting the bottle heavily again and snorting mountains of cocaine. Sharon had quit the booze completely in the wake of Randy's death, unable to tolerate the feeling of being even slightly out of control. Now engaged to be married to Ozzy once the decree nisi came through officially from Thelma, she loathed the self-abuse Ozzy indulged in but understood that this was probably not the time to try and tackle him about it. They were both, in their separate ways, doing their best to hang on. All the same, there were many nights when she simply couldn't stand it any more and – like his clothes that time in San Antonio – did her best to either hide or throw away his drugs.

'The only way I could hope to control Ozzy,' she said, 'was to literally end up having these horrendous fist fights with him all over America. Oh, God, you've no idea how many hotel rooms we destroyed with our fights,' she chortled. 'Our fights are famous among every hotel manager in America by now, I should think. The thing was, I'd discover where he'd hidden his awful bag of coke or whatever, and so I'd throw it down the toilet or out the window. Then he'd find out, and he'd beat me up, and then I'd beat him up, and it just went on and on like that for months. Randy died in March, and we were still fighting the following Christmas.'

Looking back at it years later, Ozzy could laugh about it. But the fact is he deeply resented what he saw as these intrusions into his private life. 'I'd been doing drugs since I was a teenager,' he said. 'Before that, it was booze. In my house as a kid, if you had a problem you got pissed to try and forget about it. It was as simple as that. And that's what I was trying to do now.'

He recalled one memorable occasion in his battles with Sharon when the whole thing literally exploded in his face. He and the band had just headlined a show in San Diego, in California, after which the schedule allowed for a few days off in nearby Los Angeles. Sharon and Ozzy immediately headed to one of the spacious cottages on the grounds of Don's palatial mansion for what was supposed to be a long weekend of rest and recuperation. But instead of planning a loving weekend with his fiancée, Ozzy had invited his drummer, Tommy Aldridge, to the cottage – along with a sack of coke.

'I'd bought this big, big bag of cocaine,' he told me, 'and I remember saying to myself: "This will do the old Prince of Daftness for the next three weeks!" So I'd sniffed about half this bag of coke and my eyeballs have gone like fucking traffic lights, sticking right out of my face they must have been, I was so out of it.' At which point he decided to pay a call to the main house for a chat with Don – 'which just shows you how out of it I must have been, cos Don hated drugs and if he'd known what I was doing he'd have gone fucking mad. Anyway, I went over there for a talk with him – completely out of my tree, just wanting to talk to someone about anything – and the two of us end up sitting there yakking away about his personal life. When I get back to the cottage where Sharon and I are staying, Sharon says, "Where the fuck have you been?" I said: "Talking to your father about your fucking family!" The next thing I know a plant pot comes whizzing through the window and hits me right in the head. It was Sharon! She went outside and started throwing anything she could lay her hands on at me. Then she came back inside and grabs my bag of coke and throws that out of the window too, the whole lot straight out of the window. And there was this Great Dane, who belonged to Don, walking around outside, and that fucking dog sniffed the lot. Then it started running round the house like a complete lunatic going "Whoargh! WhooOOaaARRGGHH!" All night long the dog was doing that, running round the fucking place going mad.' He paused for comic timing, then added with a straight face: 'In the end I put on a fur coat and joined it...'

'In the end,' said Sharon, listening to Ozzy tell me the story, 'I think Ozzy got so fed up with all the incredible scenes I would cause, every time I found he'd gone and scored more cocaine, I think he just wised up and refused to have anything to do with it – at least, not while I was around.' She looked at him without smiling.

Back on the road that summer it wasn't just Sharon that was beginning to find fault with Ozzy. With his reputation now extending far beyond the gossip pages of the music press and into the tabloid press, it was inevitable that their equivalent in electronic media would soon follow suit; sure enough, as Ozzy says, 'I ended up on the *David Letterman Show* in America, talking about fucking bats!' But that was as nothing compared to some of the other shows he suddenly found himself invited onto. At least the urbane Letterman was hip enough to get the joke. Elsewhere, Ozzy found himself the target of abuse from everyone from fundamental preachers like (the later disgraced) Jimmy Swaggert to evangelical TV do-gooders like Geraldo.

'I did this one TV interview with this guy who was very gentlemanly, very nice and polite before the show went live on air,' recalled Ozzy. 'The conversation went something like: "Is it fun being on the road?" I said, "Yeah, it's a bit of hard work as well". "And how's the band?" "Yeah, everyone's fine". Then we're on the air and this nice, polite, friendly man transforms before my very eyes into a fucking monster. "OZZY OSBOURNE!" "Er...yeah?" "You are supposed to be a Devil worshipper and a follower of Satan!" "Er..." "WHY DO YOU KILL POOR LITTLE ANIMALS?" Then this fruitcake interviewer turns to the camera and says: "Yes folks, this is the very person. We've got him in the studio today and we want you to know that we here at the station think this person is contemptible!" And then he wheeled in these Bible thumpers to debate with me. I tell you, I thought I was losing my mind talking to these people...'

Sharon eventually put a stop to it by refusing all requests for all such interviews after a TV appearance on the *Geraldo Show* included insert reports of human babies being boiled alive in bizarre so-called Satanic rituals. 'I mean, for fuck's sake,' she said, 'What the fuck has any of that got to with Ozzy? It was disgusting. They turned him into this pantomime villain and expected us to go along with it. In the end I told them all to fuck off.'

Out on tour, Ozzy now received death threats so regularly he was advised by security professionals to take them very seriously indeed. Security was tripled on all the remaining US dates that year, and for a time Ozzy hired a personal bodyguard, an Englishman called Big Les. Behind the scenes, however, Sharon was now facing up to what she rightly perceived as an even bigger threat to Ozzy's career: that of her own father. As she later told me: 'I'd known for years what he was like of course, but it wasn't until I started managing Ozzy that I realised just what a real bastard he could be. Mainly it was about money – Ozzy's money.' Despite his first two solo albums having now sold several million in the US alone, the old man was still withholding funds, refusing to hand over even the advances he had agreed, let alone deigning to actually fork out the voluminous royalties Ozzy was now due. And while he may have boasted that Ozzy's fee for live performances had increased 20-fold in the 18 months between his launch in the UK in November 1980 and his US tour of summer 1982, with all monies still going directly to Don's office, he was in no hurry to carve out Ozzy's slice of the pie. 'We were headlining these big places now,' said Sharon, 'and both the albums had gone platinum but we were still living more or less hand to mouth on the tour bus. Every now and then, Don would throw us a cheque. But only after I'd tell him things like Ozzy was refusing to go on until he got some money, which was a lie but was the only thing I could think of to get Don's attention. Then Randy died and everything went to hell again…'

The only bright spot on the horizon was confirmation in June that Ozzy's decree absolute had finally come through from Thelma –

leaving Ozzy free at last to marry Sharon. 'Ozzy had asked me to marry him just before we left England,' Sharon later wrote, 'when he knew that his marriage was over and that it was never going to work. I felt really bad for him. He was devastated about leaving his children, and terrified that they would turn against him and me. We were at my parents' house. And he went to H. Samuel just down the road in Wimbledon and he bought me a little diamond solitaire.'

Originally, they had planned to have a big rock'n'roll party of a wedding in England, close to their oldest friends and family. But Thelma took so long to agree a settlement – 'In the end, I gave her anything she wanted,' sighed Ozzy – they had to abandon that plan when they found themselves back on tour. Then Randy died and they no longer cared where or how they got married, just that it be soon. Said Sharon: 'At first we were going to get married in LA and then Ozzy had a tour booked in Japan, so we were in Hawaii when the decree nisi came through, so we said, "That's it, we'll get married here". And so we got married on the beach and it was lovely.'

The tour had reached Honolulu in early July. The very next day Ozzy and Sharon flew direct to the Hawaiian paradise island of Maui and booked a wedding on the beach for the morning of 4 July – American Independence Day. Booked into the Hyatt Hotel. 'It was so horrible,' Sharon later recalled, 'that Ozzy went onto the balcony and pissed on everybody below and then we checked out.' They found what they were looking for on the other side of the island: a small but elegant abode with private chalets overlooking the sea.

Ozzy's best man was Tommy Aldridge, his new best friend in the wake of Randy's death. Tommy also brought his wife Alison with him, who acted as Sharon's bridesmaid. Ozzy brought a big bag of coke and some 'Maui wowie' pot. True to form, he began his stag party 48 hours before the wedding, he and Tommy hitting several different bars and clubs dotted around the beautiful island. Ozzy was still drinking the night before the wedding when Sharon decided she was going to have an early night. She was awakened in the early hours of the morning by the phone ringing. 'It was the night porter telling me that my husband was lying in the hallway and would I go and get him,' she remembers. 'I just left him there.'

The following morning, Ozzy had sobered up enough to exchange his vows before members of both their families, including Don and his wife Paddles, and Ozzy's mother Lillian and big sister, Jean. The ceremony took place on a beachside hilltop. Sharon was 29 and Ozzy was 33. And yet the day was tinged with bittersweet moments: Sharon thinking of Rachel as she pinned her new dress back; Ozzy thinking of his children, wondering how they would take the news. To add insult to injury, Sharon recalled how, 'my mother never said a word, at least not to me, though she talked to my bridesmaid. "Oh", said Alison, looking at my mother's hand. "Sharon's wedding band is just like yours!" "Hardly", she replied. "Mine is much bigger".'

As ever Don had his own take on things. More than 20 years later he would regale me with stories of the 'sort of people' the Osbournes were, claiming he had bumped into a very distressed Ozzy before the wedding 'banging his fists against his chest.' When he enquired as to what was wrong, he claimed that Ozzy had said he was worried about inviting his mother to the wedding, that she would 'steal the fucking plates off the table!' Don said he laughed it off, then phoned ELO drummer, Bev Bevan, to be sure. Bev had been close to Ozzy and his family as a kid and told Don how 'Ozzy's mother was notorious for pulling stunts like that in the band's early days,' said Don, 'stealing the cutlery and anything else they could get their hands on' whenever they were invited to a record company do. 'What a family!' said Don, throwing up his hands. Then added, 'I went to Ozzy and told him not to worry. "Let them take all the fucking cutlery they want," I said. 'Just make sure they're there.'"

Ozzy also had the wedding cake baked to his own personal recipe, replete with several extra-strength measures of whisky. As the party reached its height, Ozzy dispensed with the local Hawaiian band and distributed their acoustic instruments to members of his own breed. The rest of the night was filled with the sound of Ozzy and the boys treating guests to a string of old Beatles' tunes, and, of all things, the song 'Goodbye To Romance' from his own *Blizzard Of Ozz* album, and, yup, 'Paranoid'.

Everyone entered into the spirit of things, sporting traditional Hawaiian garlands. Afterwards, Ozzy described it as 'the best wedding I've ever had in my life.' He was 'desperately in love with my wife and I swear to God it's the best thing that's ever happened. I'm a very proud husband.' Not proud enough though to prevent himself getting so out of it he spent his first night married to Sharon not making love but collapsed in a heap in the hotel corridor outside their room. Or as Sharon put it only half-jokingly, 'I actually carried him over the threshold.'

In truth, much as all the guests there wished the happy couple well, hardly anybody outside their immediate circle could see the marriage lasting. According to Sharon, who saw everything, 'People in the industry were taking bets. There was a big pool going – everyone was putting in £100 – six weeks, six months, nothing more than a year.'

Sharon took it all in her now practiced stride. The whole wedding had been done very much on the spur of the moment. With no time to have a proper wedding dress made, she had bought a traditional off-the-peg number from a place in LA. Far too big for her, but with her beloved Rachel no longer there to help her fix it in time, she simply pinned it in at the back. She also chose Ozzy's groom's outfit: a white suit and a lavender shirt. What did it matter that he spilled food and drink and who knows what else all over it? Forty-eight hours later they were on their way to Japan for Ozzy's first tour there as a solo artist and the wedding was just another crazy memory.

When Sharon returned to LA at the start of August, she was determined to pin her father down about the money he still owed Ozzy. For despite Don's later assertion during his time working with me that he had given Sharon Ozzy's management contract 'as a wedding present', in real terms it didn't mean much if, as Ozzy's record company chief, he was still finding ways to wheedle out of handing over the much-needed royalties, now worth several hundred thousand dollars. To add insult to injury, Sharon was presented with the news that Jet (read: Don) now wanted to release an Ozzy live album. With only two studio albums to his name as a solo artist, this seemed an unnecessarily arbitrary move on her father's part, but Sharon soon learned why. With the furore over Randy's death still making headlines, CBS (Jet's parent company) decided a posthumous live album of him performing with Ozzy was too good to be missed. Throw into the mix a selection of Black Sabbath tunes and you'd have a guaranteed No. 1 hit. Don agreed and happily accepted a sizable advance to deliver exactly that. Sharon wasn't exactly thrilled at the prospect, seeing it as possibly harmful to Ozzy's career if he were to be seen to be 'cashing in' on Randy's tragic death. However, in delivering a double album – which is what Don was proposing – it meant that, contractually at least, Ozzy would be free of Jet after that. Or so she tried to argue with the old man.

As Sharon told me, 'Don got a great deal of money to deliver an Ozzy live album. Ozzy and I eventually agreed to give Don a live album, because it was understood that as far as Ozzy's contract with Don and Jet Records was concerned, this live album would be part of our get out. After that, no more. We've actually got a complete live album's worth of material of Randy playing with Ozzy in America, but we wouldn't give that to Don. No way. Don wanted it, but after Randy's death we thought that everybody would think we were just cashing in on a tragedy, so we decided not to let Don have it under any circumstances. Then they wanted a double live album, half Ozzy solo material and half old Black Sabbath numbers, a sort of History of Ozzy Osbourne. And we said, "Fuck that, we'll just give them some old Sabbath shit, and they can take it or leave it".'

Which is exactly what happened, Ozzy hurriedly recording two consecutive shows at the fashionable Ritz Club in New York in September, where he and the band played nothing but Black Sabbath-era material. No one was pleased with the final product – the live double, *Talk of the Devil* – not Ozzy nor Don, certainly not Jet or CBS and not even Sharon, but it did the trick in terms of getting Ozzy out of Don's clutches. Or as Ozzy said: 'I hate that fucking so-called Ozzy live album. That ain't an Ozzy live album, that's an obligation I fulfilled in order to get me out of a very bad situation.' So upset was he by this latest turn of events, Ozzy tried to get out of the whole thing – by shaving his head completely bald.

'I woke up one morning and he was gone,' Sharon remembered. 'He was gone the whole day and all the next night. By this time I'm freaking out wondering where on earth he's gone. I've rung up the police and had him listed as an official missing person, I'm going out of my mind with worry. The next morning I wake up and he's standing there with this horrible green woollen hat pulled down over his ears, and he is trembling all over. I ask him where the hell does he think he's been for the last 24 hours and he just mumbles and fumbles around. And he won't take this blasted hat off. In the end, he pulled if off and there he was – completely fucking bald with a horrible sorry look on his face. I could have died! He was under so much pressure at that point from Don that he just freaked out.'

As usual, however, once she'd gotten over the shock, Sharon did what she always did and took the whole thing in her ever-lengthening stride. Determined the show must go on at any cost – reasoning that the sooner the album was out, the sooner they could escape her father – she went out the same day and bought Ozzy a range of wigs he could wear for the shows. Sure enough, he did the New York shows, turning his baldness into a feature by yanking the wig off halfway through the set each night – to the utter astonishment of the audience who assumed it was all part of the act and simply applauded even louder. Truly, he really was the madman of rock!

'I didn't want to know anything about those fucking gigs,' said Ozzy when we spoke about it later. 'But I was under horrendous pressure to do them, just so as I could get away from Don Arden. I'd finally realised that the man was not interested in my career. He didn't give a damn when I left Sabbath and even now when I was doing so well on my own, he still had absolutely no fucking imagination. He wanted me out on that road, releasing albums that didn't mean a thing left right and centre, and if it was left to him my career would be over before it had even really begun. Fuck that.'

For Sharon, however, there were even more serious reasons for wanting a complete break from her father, and none of them musical. Or even much to do with Ozzy. As she later put it to me, 'I knew the war was about to start and I wanted to get as far away as possible before it did...'

Act II
Scene Four:

Fuck the World

Don Arden was absolutely adamant: none of it was his fault. It was all her: the she-devil he had reared. In his eyes he was entirely the innocent party, she the evil schemer who had plotted against him. And after all he'd done for her – this was how she thanked him? What father truly deserved that?

'By the time she married Ozzy, I could already see where this was going. I knew it wasn't just Ozzy as a husband she was after. I mean, I don't doubt she loved him – she must have done to put up with him. But would she have fallen in love with him if he'd been the postman? No. She had her sights set on controlling his career, too. I thought, what's the point in trying to stop her? If he's going to marry her she's going to take him anyway. So I went and got the [management] contract from the safe and put it in an envelope and wrote her name on it. Then I gave it to her and said, "This is my wedding present to you both. I hope it brings you great success and happiness".'

It was an entirely selfless action on the part of a loving, caring father he said, looking to do something to really set the marriage on its way. As Don put it: 'A happy ending for all.' Instead, he said, wrinkling his nose and fixing me with those cold fish eyes, 'it turned out to be just the beginning. One bad move led to another and the whole thing turned into a catastrophe. Sharon and I did not speak to each other again for over 20 years. Not without fighting anyway.' It was 'war,' he said and it was 'to the death.' At least as far as Sharon was concerned. Dear old Don would have done anything to avoid it, he said. Loved her still, he said. But she wouldn't have it. All the bad blood between them, the threats and court actions and violent outbursts when they did see each other, the conniving and backstabbing and lies and hate, it was all down to her. He said.

On the train going home from my latest meeting with Don, I would sometimes think of the times, 20 years before, when Sharon had first spoken to me about her father. How for many years she had been 'terrified of him.' The times, she said, when he phoned and warned her he was on his way round to see her. 'There were times when I was on the floor crying and shaking because he'd threatened to come over to the house and kill me,' she once told me. 'He's an evil old bastard and I can't wait for him to die.'

So what actually happened? Many things, it seemed. On a general level, it seems the alarming breakdown in relations between daddy and daddy's girl had been coming for some time. By the time Sharon was in her mid-twenties and working for her father full-time, he had devised several tried-and-trusted tricks to 'save money', as he put it – or avoid paying back bank loans, record company advances, royalties, tax, or any other 'nuisance' creditor. Chiefly, this now involved putting his various companies into the name of others: principally, his wife and children; more often than not, Sharon, who, sensing perhaps she would not wish to know the answers anyway, tended not to ask too many awkward questions, then or later.

By the start of the eighties, however, a great many of Don's chickens were coming home to roost it seemed. When, in the past, this might have meant being chased by debt collectors, both Sharon and David had become adept at helping the old man fob people off. This was more serious. Sharon was flabbergasted – and caught horribly on the wrong foot – when ELO singer-songwriter Jeff Lynne sat her down one night and calmly explained that Don owed him personally in the region of $4 million. She had grown used to her father's artists crying foul at various points, she had also seen him turn them into huge stars. But this was different. Jeff had always been a reasonable guy. She knew he wasn't lying or trying to get one over on her. When even she began to suffer from Don's financial trans-gressions as Ozzy's manager, she realised her father was 'a hypocrite.' Not only that but 'a fucking thief.'

Still, though, she continued to work beneath his giant and forbidding shadow. Then something happened that went beyond financial considerations, something which so blew her mind there was simply no way back in it for her father. She discovered he was having an affair. Not just a one-off sexual shenanigan with a professional hostess, perhaps, the kind of which she had been aware since she discovered her father always kept a private suite for such activities at the Beverly Hills Hotel, but a serious, ongoing love affair with an American woman named Meredith Goodwin. For Sharon, this was the last straw. Not because of what it might do to her mother, who she had never been as close to as she had been to her father, but because of what it said about him and his relationship with his daughter. Used to the old man looking down his nose at others who kept mistresses, acting as judge and jury on anyone he felt hadn't acted to his own deeply moral code of conduct – even when he used it to justify beating and torturing them – she simply couldn't get her head round the fact that he was now one of them: a two-faced, adulterous middle-aged millionaire who not only ripped off people in business including his own daughter, but appeared to revel in it too. Finally, she said, 'My world had shattered.'

'Sharon was just jealous,' said Don when we broached the subject one day. 'She wanted me all to herself.' I looked at him, unsure exactly what he meant. Don liked to just throw things out there. Like his daughter and son-in-law, he had a fondness for saying things just to see the effect they would have. He studied my face to see if his words were having the desired effect. 'She loved me too much, that's all.' he said. Well, she is your daughter, I ventured. 'Yes,' he sneered. 'But it was more than that.' More? 'Yes.' Just then David came in and overheard what the old man was saying. He sighed heavily. 'For God's sake dad, don't start all that again.' Don leaned back in his chair and laughed. 'It's true, though,' he said. Dave frowned. 'For God's sake...'

That was the thing about Don. He loved playing the wicked old man. The thing about Sharon was that she loved playing the daughter of the wicked old man. There was no doubt though that he had hurt her – and, eventually, she him. The only thing that was crystal clear was that only one of them was really prepared to acknowledge it, and it was never going to be the old man. Not in front of me anyway.

In retrospect, however, it's tempting to see this rift between father and daughter as the beginning of the end for one – Don – and the start of something incredibly big for the other – Sharon. Maybe it was just that his time was up. With Jeff Lynne now suing him for unpaid monies, ELO, his prime asset, were also in the throes of disentangling themselves from his tentacles. Once Sharon had taken the official step of informing CBS – Jet's paymasters – that she too would be suing Don for back payments and that Ozzy would no longer be recording for him, it was another massive blow, to his ego and most of all his pocket. Within a year he had sold the Howard Hughes mansion and most of its contents and set up a much smaller home with Meredith in Century City, a pleasant enclave of LA but hardly the hub of activity the way the old house and grounds had been. Though he continued to manage his own label and even took charge of another multi-platinum rock act in Air Supply, his days as the great music biz shark were largely over. Or maybe it was something else.

According to David, Don essentially gave up his family and business for Meredith. He said his father had 'become so obsessed with her' that nothing else really mattered. He certainly seemed to find something in his relationship with Meredith he'd never had – or thought he'd never had – before. As he told me, 'They say opposites attract and I liked it that she knew nothing about my business, my world. Her own life was so different.' Meredith was 'a successful academic.' Her father had been 'one of the top engineers at NASA during the space programme in the sixties.' Meredith didn't know anything about rock'n'roll, or what Don had done to get where he was. She was a lady who treated him like a gentleman. Having spent his whole life reinventing himself – a character trait his daughter would inherit and enlarge on to even greater extent – it appeared he had one last incarnation he wished to invoke. That of well-to-do businessman, cultivated and semi-retired, a good egg from a now long-forgotten nest. America was full of such people: bad guys done good. Why not Don Arden – Harry Levy – too?

Sharon wasn't having it. The first time she saw the two of them together – having lunch in the Polo Lounge of the Beverly Hills Hotel – she marched straight over and tipped Meredith's bowl of soup over her. Don sighed as he recounted the tale. 'You couldn't convince Sharon that this wasn't the right way for a lady to behave in public.' Don just couldn't understand it, he said. What had he done wrong? Even Paddles was happy for him, he said. Ten years older than her husband, their relationship had 'reached a very advanced level of understanding.' No longer living in LA anyway, she now spent her days at Kimberley House, the home he had bought her in Dorking, Surrey, where David and his family also lived whenever they were in England. While Meredith gave him 'youthful companionship and all the excitement that goes with it.'

That's not how Sharon remembers it though. In her own auto-biography, *Extreme*, she recalls how her mother only found out about Meredith during a brief visit to the house in LA, when, to her astonishment, she actually discovered a prenuptial agreement between Don and Meredith while hunting for something else in a drawer. Her mother later confided in Sharon that she'd known Don was a serial adulterer for years but that it was something she 'turned a blind eye to.' She had lost her first husband through his philandering ways; she was not prepared to lose another, not least so late in life. Nevertheless, writes Sharon, there were many times over the next few years when her mother 'would call me, crying on the phone.' Sharon was dragged into becoming the 'go-between – the voice that she didn't have. The raging bull that she wished she was.' In the end it was all too much for her and she cut off relations with both her parents. These were dark times but by now Sharon and Ozzy had their own family to worry about. Unable to cope, she simply refused to acknowledge she even had a father and mother. Something she would later regret deeply. There was no time for such thoughts now, though, in 1982, as Ozzy's career hung in the balance.

'As soon as Don knew we were leaving him,' Sharon told me, 'the shit hit the fan.' According to Don he was 'forced' to sue both Sharon and Ozzy because they had 'broken their contract with me'. He may have 'given' Sharon Ozzy's management contract but that didn't mean he would allow her to take Ozzy away from his record company, Jet, without a fight. According to Sharon, though, she simply 'had no choice. We were broke and it was the only way we were ever going to get our money.' No, said Don, he had never tried to rip anyone off, least of all his daughter and new son-in-law. In fact, 'it was the opposite. Sharon was trying to do me.' No, said Sharon, 'It was the only way I knew we could get away from him.' In fact she said, she was 'terrified of what he might do.' He had already tried to talk Ozzy into getting the marriage annulled, she claimed, less than a month after the wedding, confiding in Ozzy that his daughter, sadly, was 'insane.' But not even Ozzy, drunk as he was at the time, believed that. 'I knew it was all kicking off between them,' he told me, 'and I didn't want nothing to do with it, I wasn't getting in the middle of that, old bean, do you know what I mean? One thing I did know though was that Sharon was the only one looking out for me. Don was always nice to me but she was the one who really cared.'

By the time I had gotten to know both Sharon and Ozzy in 1985, the situation with Don had at least been resolved on paper – a settlement worth over a million dollars reached, in which it was agreed that Don be paid off for his services and Ozzy be free to continue his career with another label (Epic) and another manager (Sharon) – but that didn't mean the war was over yet. Even though Don was now living with Meredith and still successful, while Ozzy and Sharon were at last being paid the money they earned together directly, not via Don's grasping hands, the bitterness between the two sides was still palpable whenever the subject was raised, as it invariably was on a weirdly regular basis. Any chance Sharon got, she would put the old man down. Any chance Don got, he would try and stick the knife into his daughter. It didn't matter what the circumstances were, the blood between them continued to be badder than bad.

Even when Ozzy agreed to reunite with Black Sabbath to perform at the America end of Live Aid, it involved a convoluted sideshow in which father once again tried to 'get one over' his daughter. Now acting as Ozzy's official biographer, Sharon had flown me to Philadelphia for the concert, too, and I got to see the whole sorry saga unfold. The day before the show, Ozzy had been sitting outside the Four Seasons hotel where we were all staying doing a TV interview to promote the show when suddenly out of nowhere an officious looking dude stepped in front of the camera and served him with papers: an injunction from Don.

In the wake of losing Ozzy to Sharon, Don had returned to being Sabbath's manager. The band and their new singer Ronnie James Dio had been remarkably successful in their initial post-Ozzy period. But then Dio left too and their career began to nosedive. Fans will accept one singer leaving, perhaps, but two...? No. Ozzy's career, meanwhile, had gone from strength to strength, to the point where his next album, *The Ultimate Sin*, would be his biggest hit, with or without Sabbath. A galling situation for his old band, still managed by Don. When the offer from Bob Geldof for the reunited band to make a 15-minute appearance at Live Aid was made, Sharon only agreed to it on the strict condition that her father was not within a hundred miles of the event on the day. Desperate to get back into the spotlight, and secretly hoping for a longer-term reconciliation with Ozzy, the rest of the band had been happy to agree. Don was incandescent with rage and decided to act in the only way he knew how: as Sharon put it, 'to try and fuck it up for everybody.'

It hadn't worked though, as Sharon's lawyers furiously batted back the would-be injunction and the show went ahead as planned. Ozzy and Sabbath were due on stage at the stunningly inappropriate time of 10.00am. That morning as we stood in the lobby waiting for our ride to the JFK Stadium where the event was taking place, Ozzy was in understandably downbeat mood. 'I know it's for a good cause,' he said about the show, 'but to be honest, I don't really care.' Being back with Sabbath – the band that had effectively left him behind to die – was traumatic enough, he said. But he'd gotten over that the minute they'd all started rehearsing together. The business with Don had taken the wind out of his sails, though. 'It's like my father used to say: in the war, everyone was friendly and helped each other, but as soon as the war ended they were back to being pricks again. And I bet there'll be people there tomorrow who'll be telling each other to go fuck themselves again the next day.'

Sharon was battling with her own mixed feelings. It wasn't just her father that was getting her down. In order for Ozzy to do the show it meant her having to work with Black Sabbath again, something she did not relish for all sorts of private and professional reasons, least of all as it entailed having to be in the same room as Tony Iommi again. In the wake of the split from Ozzy – and her father retaking control of Sabbath – there had been a lot of bad blood between the two camps that seemed to extend beyond the war raging between Don and Sharon. When Ozzy brought a dwarf into his act – which was ritually 'hanged' each night on stage – and nicknamed him 'Ronnie' it was

161

perceived as a sideswipe at the singer who had replaced Ozzy in Sabbath: Ronnie James Dio, a famously short person with a giant-sized hang-up about his height. Then, when Sabbath released an album in 1983 titled *Born Again* and chose an album cover that depicted a newborn baby as the spawn of the Devil, replete with fangs and horns and an evil grimace, it got back to Sharon that Iommi and the others had nicknamed it 'Aimee' – in reference to Sharon and Ozzy's daughter Aimee, born the same year.

'I just thought they were sick,' she told me. 'It's one thing to call each other names and take the piss. It's another to drag someone's child into it. I thought, I'll teach you, you bastards.' Seeing Iommi as the ringleader, she persuaded a friend of hers – 'a famous model' – to call the guitarist at the studio where he was working one night and introduce herself, then explain that she had always been an enormous Black Sabbath fan and would like to meet him. 'To make it sound more convincing, I got her to tell him to look in *Vogue* to see a picture of her – and you have to imagine, she was stunning. So of course Iommi took one look and immediately started panting. Then I got her to arrange to meet him for dinner at Le Dome', a famous restaurant in LA. Sure enough, said Sharon, Iommi had turned up 'in his best leather jacket with all the little crosses on it,' she sneered. Only when he got there, there was no beautiful model waiting for him, just an empty table. As he ordered himself a drink and settled back for his date to turn up, however, Sharon's chauffeur walked in carrying a Tiffany box. 'I had it all arranged,' she chortled. 'The box was done up in ribbons with a little card on it, signed: Love, Sharon and Ozzy.' When Iommi opened the box, inside were 'two great big fresh turds,' Sharon laughed: 'One from Ozzy and one from me.'

Now on the day of the show, Sharon found a reason not to travel down to the stadium with Ozzy and the band. In fact, when I bumped into her she was talking to Ozzy's American PR, Michael Jensen, about another matter: Ozzy's imminent cosmetic surgery. Michael had reluctantly been explaining that several news reporters had remarked to him off the record about how much weight Ozzy appeared to be carrying. And it was true; he was certainly looking heavier than he had been in Rio just six months before. 'Don't worry about that,' Sharon reassured the nervous PR. 'We're taking care of all that before the next album.' She looked at me and smiled: 'I just wish I could take care of myself too.' As she was then heavily pregnant, I took this to be a joke about her nervousness at the imminent birth. 'These women that say they want natural births,' she said, 'I don't understand it. When I give birth I want all the fucking drugs they can give me. And so would you, if you had to go through something like that!'

Later, though, it became clear that Sharon had been referring to more than that when she talked about wishing she could join Ozzy and 'take care of myself too.' Sharon wasn't the kind to be self-conscious or apologetic about things like cosmetic surgery, though she was canny enough to realise that any 'work' Ozzy had done would best be kept quiet as his teenage fans wouldn't see things quite the same. However, she was terribly self-conscious about her own body shape. While Ozzy turned to drink and drugs to help him with his stress, Sharon would turn to comfort eating, which in recent years had turned to binge eating. She'd done 'the whole health farm and crash diet thing,' she said but all to no avail. 'You might lose a few pounds while you're doing it but it all comes back the minute you stop.' Even though Ozzy affected not to notice or care, it was clearly getting Sharon down. Something would have to be done sooner or later, she said, 'or I'm gonna explode.' I could only concur. Earlier during the trip when Sharon had mentioned she was pregnant, I had shown my surprise – tempered, I hoped with delight – and congratulated her heartily. It was only afterwards that one of her assistants whispered in my ear: 'You fool! She's seven months pregnant!' Blimey, I said. She was so…um…*large* anyway, I hadn't realised. Oh…

It seemed like a strange conversation to be having on the morning of Live Aid – a concert designed to 'feed the world' but then we weren't really talking about food. We were talking about depression, fear, stress and a degree of self-loathing. I was surprised. It was the first time I realised, in my youthful foolishness, that for all her millions, someone like Sharon Osbourne could still be deeply unhappy about certain key aspects of her life.

I walked back out to where Ozzy and the others were hanging around the lobby, still thinking it over. Then the minibus arrived and we climbed in. Just as the doors were closing a middle-aged man with fair hair and long rockabilly sideburns jumped in. We all moved up one and the van drove off.

'I'm Martin Chambers, by the way,' he announced.

'Oh, aye,' said Bill Ward.

'You know? From The Pretenders?'

'Oh, aye. What do *you* do?'

'I'm the drummer.'

'Oh, aye.'

We fell into silence. It was still so early; none of us was really awake yet. But Martin couldn't help himself. He leaned across the seat. 'You're Ozzy Osbourne, aren't you?'

Ozzy eyed him disinterestedly. 'That's right, mate.'

'So the rest of you must be Black Sabbath,' he said, grinning. No one grinned back. So he tried again, an affable sort of bloke, just no good at reading situations. 'I've always loved that song you did…"Paranoid", is it?'

Ozzy nodded. Martin still didn't get it. Just sensed he'd gone wrong somewhere. Wow, these heavy metal guys, they're so weird!

One more go. 'So what are you doing, just three numbers like the rest of us?'

'That's right,' said Ozzy with a straight face. 'But we've got a special surprise worked out for them. For an encore we're gonna come on and do "Food Glorious Food".'

The band began to titter. Martin looked puzzled. Still game, but starting to wonder. Then Ozzy broke into song: 'Food glorious food! Hot sausage tomato!'

Everyone joined in. Everyone except Martin. When that finished Bill asked Ozzy how Sharon – now heavily pregnant – was getting on. Ozzy said she was fine but joked there was no way he was going to be there for the birth this time. Not after the last time with Kelly. 'Fuck me!' he roared. 'They tell you all about being there to hold the old lady's hand and help her breathe and all this shit, and then you get there and it's like a scene from the fucking *Exorcist*! Blood and fucking guts everywhere! The doctors were on about giving her drugs for the pain, I was like, fuck that, give 'em to me! You fucking need something to get you through that, I tell you!'

Martin looked at him and blinked, went to say something then thought better of it and shut up. Like most people that didn't know him, he couldn't figure out if Ozzy was joking or not. Even those of us that did know him didn't always have the answer to that one, though.

165

Sabbath's actual performance that morning was bizarre. They just didn't have the right save-the-world type songs. 'Children of the Grave' was the closest they got and even that felt ridiculously heavy-handed. While anyone who could tell you what 'Iron Man' or 'Paranoid' had to do with starving Africans, even in the wildest, most metaphorical sense, would have to have been a serious philosopher. Or simply taking the piss.

Ozzy, in particular, who hadn't sung live since Rock in Rio six months before, looked like he was struggling. Overweight and over-dressed in the far too bright morning sun, he was all chins and puffiness, out of breath and out of sync. Then, suddenly, it was over, the band had done their bit to feed the world even if it did feel like they were stuffing it down their faces. 'I looked like a fat Joan Collins,' Ozzy moaned all the way back to the hotel. 'Like Mama Cass at a gay party!'

That afternoon, back at the Four Seasons, Ozzy and I sat together in the hotel bar, the concert playing on the huge TV screen on the wall beside us. With Ozzy once again on the wagon that meant I was too and there was simply nothing else but to sit and chat. This being America, and today having been about Black Sabbath, Ozzy's mind wandered back to the first time he'd ever toured here with the band, back in 1971.

Back then America was 'the dream for any band. It didn't matter where you were in the charts, if you could say you'd been to America, you'd really made it, in my book,' he smiled. 'I remember when I eventually got on the plane to go to America, we flew with Stevie Winwood and Traffic, and it was like, whoa! The Rock Star Express! I thought all big rock stars must fly on the same plane. Then we got to the hotel in New York, this shit-hole on 8th and 48th Street, and I had my first experience of silicone tits. The manager had got a load of these slags around and I remember knocking on the adjoining door to Tony's room and going, "Fucking hell, Tony, you want to see what I've got in bed, it looks like the winner of the 3.30 from Kelso." He said, "You think that's bad, look at the fucking thing in my room!"'

I laughed but he kept up the same doleful expression he always did when telling one of his stories, somewhere between Buster Keaton and Eeyore. 'I swear, other bands' roadies got better-looking groupies than we did. They would be so bad you'd have to put a bag over their heads. The really bad ones we called Two-Baggers. One bag for her head, to stop you seeing what you were doing, and one bag for your head – in case anyone came in, so they wouldn't know it was you. In England in them days, if you wanted to fuck a chick you'd wine her and dine her and maybe three weeks later you'd pop the question. Forget it, baby, they ain't got time for that in America. The chicks would walk up and go, "I wanna ball you," and I'd think, "What the fuck does that mean?"' In those days, he said, 'the groupies knew more about our tour itineraries than we did. Gigs, bars, hotels, radio interviews…they were everywhere we went. We suffered the results as well. We got clap, crabs, all sorts of different diseases. Then we'd have to go through the cures, big painful shots of penicillin in the arse…'

Having been researching their story for the book about him I was to shortly write, I told Ozzy how I'd been interested to discover that, unlike Britain, where the music press affected indifference to their music, in America Sabbath had actually found themselves critically fêted – at least, in the early days. *Creem* magazine's legendary editor, Lester Bangs, was an early champion, memorably describing them in 1972 as 'moralists' and comparing their lyrics to those of Bob Dylan and the books of William Burroughs. Not everybody agreed. Andrew Weiner wrote in *Rock File* that, 'Black Sabbath relates to casual street-fighting and mind-numbing boredom…to the entire depressing English working class experience.' American critics called it 'downer music'; the perfect soundtrack to the Quaaludes-and-red wine generation of Vietnam draftees-in-waiting that attended Sabbath's US shows in the early seventies.

He looked at me like he didn't know what the fuck I was talking about. 'We never really took it that serious,' he said. 'Well, I didn't, the others might have. Maybe Geezer when he was writing lyrics or whatever. We just used to take the piss. Geezer would say things in *Rolling Stone* like being the seventh son of a seventh son and all that. I used to say I'd be dead before I was 40. Mind you, I probably would have been if it hadn't been for Sharon…'

I told him that I'd also read that legendary record producer and general LA bon viveur Kim Fowley once told Ozzy he should go to Mexico and buy a corpse, then take it on stage and stab it. 'You what? Fuck off, that never happened. No, wait…*maybe*. I'll tell you what I do remember,' he said. 'At that time in America, too, people were very fond of lacing your drinks with acid. I didn't care. I used to swallow handfuls of acid tabs at a time. The end of it came when we got back to England. I took 10 tabs of acid then went for a walk in a field. I ended up standing there talking to this horse for about an hour. In the end, the horse turned round and told me to fuck off. That was it for me…'

We sat there, continuing to watch the concert on the TV. 'The thing is,' he said, 'they'll get the money, and food will be taken over and they'll feed them and they'll *still* fucking starve again because the food, no matter how much is raised today, won't last forever. I think that not only rock'n'roll groups should do this, but industry, too – the IBMs and GECs. They should say, "All right, one week a year our output will go to charity", whatever that might be. I mean, they spend hundreds of millions on nuclear defence, but would they ever say, "OK, let's save a hundred million today and feed these fuckers"? That's nothing to the government; it's not a piss in the ocean. It's like giving a tramp a dime. But no, they'd rather burn leftover supplies of wheat than stop people dying. They crush billions and billions of apples back into the ground because of surplus stocks...I mean, I know it's only apples and they'd probably be bored stiff sitting back in the old desert eating a ton of fucking apples, but it's better than a fucking pile of dirt, ain't it?'

What Ozzy and Sabbath were getting out of it though, was harder to tell. A place in the history books? Or was there something else cooking? Was the band planning to do like Deep Purple had the year before and cash in with a big reformation tour? An appearance on the bill at Live Aid would certainly have been the perfect platform for making such an announcement.

He looked shocked at the very thought. 'No fucking way, mate!' he shook his head. I pushed him for more. He rambled on a bit and then he finally got to it. 'At the end of the day, I have to ask myself, if Black Sabbath had done as well as I'm doing now and kept hold of Ronnie Dio in the group or whatever, and I was where they left me, down and out in a fucking LA bar, would they give everything up just to bring me back into the group?'

He looked at me. Well, we both knew the answer to that one. 'Christ,' he said, 'do you know how many years it took me to get *out* of that fucking mess with Sabbath? And all these cunts who *do* get back together, don't ever believe that it's for any reason other than the fucking money. If there *was* another reason, they'd never have called each other cunts and split up in the first place. No, bollocks to all that! I've got enough to worry about trying to kick this drink thing, you know?'

How was he getting on with that, I wondered? 'I've still got me own bar at home,' he told me. 'Except it's got no booze in it now. It's all Diet Cokes now, and I ask you, what's the good of having your own bar at home if you can't have any beer in it? It's like having a dartboard with no darts! That's what my life is now,' he said, looking around, 'a pool table with no balls…'

As he once told me, 'I know I'm no fucking brain surgeon. I'm not what you'd call a really *heavy* songwriter. I'm not even that great a singer. It's not exactly what I'm known for, put it that way. With me, it's all the other stuff – the mad fucking stuff. That's what people think of when they think of me. Biting the head off a fucking bat! Getting pissed and getting stoned and arrested…all the crazy stuff. I don't mind. I only mind when they go on about devil-worshipping and all that fucking crap. That really does my fucking head in that does. Other than that, they can say what they fucking well like, mate. It's probably true, most of it, anyway…'

Act II
Scene Five:

We've Decided

If the original 1969 Woodstock festival, with its gruesomely naked bodies, uninhibited drug-taking and unprecedented approach to crowd control – come on down, brothers and sisters, it's all free! – had been emblematic of the countercultural 'revolution' of the late sixties, there can have been no better symbol of the money-grabbing, drug-hypocritical, so-called safe sex 1980s than the Moscow Music Peace Festival, held in August 1989, exactly 20 years and what seemed like several lifetimes later. Never mind Live Aid. More people may remember that but Live Aid, with its ultra-focused fundraising and dizzying global clout, was more of a hand-holding sixties throwback than it was a genuine expression of the age; a cultural aberration that deliberately traded on 'me-first' eighties guilt to ram home its almost anachronistic message: feed the children, help the poor, pretend Thatcher and Reagan never existed (and while you're at it, help revive my career).

The Moscow Music Peace Festival, however, was a genuinely self-absorbed, glossed-over, height-of-the-eighties, multimedia event;

inspired by the deeply held desire of a convicted international drug-trafficker to avoid going to jail, and the fervent wishes of the famous bands whose careers he then guided not to be robbed of their Svengali, their bad daddy, their real money-maker. In short, the only interests the Moscow Music Peace Festival really served were of the people on the stage, not the ones off it.

Even the location for the event seemed bizarrely at odds with prevailing rock culture, certainly as it had existed up until 1989: since when had the Lenin Stadium in Moscow become a venue-of-choice for high-profile rock bands?

Since Doc McGhee said so, that's when. McGhee was then manager of five of the seven big-name bands that would appear on the Moscow bill: Bon Jovi, the Scorpions, Mötley Crüe, Skid Row and local Russian outfit Gorky Park. While the only other big name acts appearing at the festival not connected to McGhee – Ozzy Osbourne and Cinderella – were both managed by people he'd worked with many times over the years (notably, Sharon Osbourne, on the Crüe's breakthrough US tour opening for Ozzy six years before, and when Doc returned the favour by letting Lita Ford, then managed by Sharon, open for Bon Jovi on his 1988 world tour). McGhee was also a convicted felon. Or as drummer Tommy Lee later put it in the official Mötley Crüe biography, *The Dirt*: 'Before [McGhee] met us, he was living a secret life that blew up on him when he got busted for helping smuggle forty thousand fucking pounds of pot from Colombia into North Carolina. It wasn't his only bust, because he was also being accused of associating with some well-connected madmen who had conspired to bring over a half a million pounds of blow [cocaine] and weed into the United States in the early-eighties.'

The result, after he had pleaded guilty at the trial in North

Carolina, was a relatively modest $15,000 fine, plus a five-year suspended prison sentence. The reason he was able to get off with such a light sentence was his additional offer to put together an anti-drugs organisation, the Make A Difference Foundation, for which he would raise money the only legal way he knew how: via his music biz connections. As Tommy said: 'Doc knew that anyone else probably would have been in jail for at least 10 years for that shit, so he had to do something high-profile to show the court he was doing the world some good as a free man. And his brainstorm was to commemorate the 20th anniversary of Woodstock with the Moscow Music Peace Festival.' But as Tommy ruefully concluded: 'It was all bad from the moment we stepped on the plane…There was a so-called doctor on board, who was plying the bands who weren't sober with whatever medicine they needed. It was clear that this was going to be a monumental festival of hypocrisy.'

Not that I was yet aware of any of that as I stood there, sweaty and starving, at Sheremetyevo Airport in August 1989, waiting for the plane to land. I was still too flummoxed by Moscow itself to worry about what any of the bands might be thinking. I had arrived 48 hours before to find a Moscow gripped by such a fearful heat that all the sensible (read: rich) people had fled the city for their summer dachas. Not that there was much to keep them there during the cooler months anyway. Back then, before the Berlin Wall had fallen, the image Moscow conjured up in one's mind was of a large, grey, unhappy citadel full of long faces and even longer food queues. The reality, however, was much worse than that. Rule number one, I discovered on my first night there, was There Is No Food. That is, nothing edible. There were restaurants, of course, but mostly they were all closed. Usually for 'cleaning', which seemed to take place approximately six nights out of seven. Even when you did find a restaurant open it invariably wasn't worth eating in. Learning to survive on the road means learning to eat anything. Fussy eaters are the first to throw in the towel. Never in all my travels, though, had I come across anything so frankly – or ironically – vomit-inducing as the Chicken Kiev in Russia. 'Why do you think there are no dogs on the streets of Moscow?' whispered Dimitri, conspiratorially – one of the many official KGB-approved festival 'guides' and 'interpreters' – as I pushed away my plate again one night.

Rule number two: There Is No Such Thing as Russian Money. Well, actually, there was – it was called the rouble, but no self-respecting Russian trader would accept them as currency. Officially, a rouble was the equivalent of £1. But on the black market, you could get up to 10 roubles for your pound. Even then, however, they simply weren't worth having. The only thing a stack of roubles could buy you was a wooden doll and a big furry hat. The only real consumer goods available were on sale in the tourist-only stores, which took all major credit cards, including American Express. In fact, the main currency in Moscow back then, spookily, was US dollars. And if you didn't have the exact amount you could throw in a pack of Marlboros. For change, you might receive an assortment of dollar bills, 10-franc pieces and the occasional silver Deutsche Mark. For small change you might get handed a packet of orange-flavoured Tic-Tacs. No joke.

As for music…well, these days, no doubt, it's as easy in Moscow to download your favourites from the Internet as it is anywhere else. Back then, however, records and tapes were purchased almost exclusively on the black market. There was only one official record store in the whole of Moscow and when I visited it they were selling the sort of junk you might find at a car boot sale – dusty Frank Ifield

LPs and third-generation homemade cassettes of The Beatles. Everything else was either banned or simply not available in the Russian market.

Along with most of the Western bands flying in for the festival, I was staying at a 'five star' tourist hotel in the heart of Moscow, one block from Red Square and the imposing shadow of the Kremlin. Old and remarkably unattractive prostitutes lined the entrance to the hotel and dark-suited security guards with the thick necks and thicker accents of Bond villains checked the ID of everyone wishing to enter. Enormous black cockroaches clung lazily to the walls and ceiling of the lobby. In my room on the 16th floor, I was advised by one of the advance crew to check for bedbugs before turning in for the night. In my bathroom the water running from the taps was the rich brown colour of yesterday's piss; in the soap dish there sat a decomposing apple-core. The only towel provided was hanky-thin and crisp as an old rag. Two cigarette stubs floated lifelessly in the toilet pan. I was truly baffled. What the fuck had happened back there when they'd had the Great Revolution? Hadn't anybody come out on top at the end of it? And if they had, where did those guys go to eat – and sleep? I had only been in bed 10 minutes when there was a knock at my door. I thought it might be the KGB. But when I opened the door a crack there was only one of the grotesque prostitutes from the lobby, asking if I'd like to buy champagne ('Only 10 dollars, US,' she grinned uninvitingly) or perhaps more ('I keep you company, yes?' Er, no…thanks).

This happened every single night I was there. On the third night, already drunk and feeling emboldened after another day of dog-burgers and Tic-Tacs, I invited her in. She asked if she could bring a friend and out of nowhere an even larger, much uglier woman appeared. I gave them $20 and we opened a couple of bottles of champagne. It was so sickly sweet it made Asti Spumanti taste like Dom Perignon. I sat there on the bed morosely, drinking it and asking them about Russia. They agreed that Russian life was 'verrry bad.' Never mind, I said, Gorbachev was working on it, right? 'No!' they cried in unison. Gorbachev was 'verrry, verry bad!' They said they'd preferred life under the old regime. At least, then, they said, you could get meat and bread and didn't have to queue for everything. I gave them another $20 when they left and went to sleep feeling worse than ever. Gorby may have been a huge hero to the West back then but apparently he didn't mean shit to the ordinary whores and champagne guzzlers of Moscow. I went to sleep thinking I understood but of course I didn't.

It goes without saying that the bands were even more nonplussed when they arrived. Walking through Red Square in the rain with Ozzy the day after he landed, he looked around glumly and summed up the general feeling surrounding the build-up to the festival when he said: 'If I was living here full time, I'd probably be dead of alcoholism, or sniffing car tyres – anything to get out of it. I can understand why there's such an alcohol problem here. There's nothing else to do.'

It was true. But then, Ozzy was one of the acts on the bill still struggling with the 'substance abuse' issues the festival was supposed to be helping tackle. He gave a hollow laugh as he told me about the case of Russian vodka the local promoter had presented to him on his arrival. 'They talk about how much this show is going to help the poor cunts who get drunk out of their minds here every night,' he said, 'then stand there waiting for you to get shit-faced with them on their special bloody vodka. It don't make sense. It don't to me anyway. What do you reckon?'

I reckoned I couldn't wait to leave. It seemed Ozzy was even more keen on leaving when I heard later the same day that he was threatening to pull out of the event after McGhee suddenly changed his placing on the bill from third to fourth, upgrading Mötley Crüe to the slot above Ozzy. McGhee took the threat seriously enough to return Ozzy to his original placing on the bill, just below the Scorpions and Bon Jovi, and Ozzy kept his promise and did the show. 'I didn't give a fuck, to be honest,' Ozzy told me later. 'It was Sharon putting her foot down. The thing is, she agreed for me to come here in exchange for certain things, like where I would appear on the bill and all that – normal management type stuff. Then Doc started fucking around with things and she went ballistic. As you know, if there's one thing you don't wanna do with my old lady is start trying to fuck her around. Doc might think he's a tough guy but he's got nothing on Sharon, mate. Fuck all…'

The last time I saw Ozzy had been in Red Square, still looking for a way out. 'Have you discovered any of the night life here yet?' he asked me disinterestedly. I shook my head. He seemed relieved. The last thing he wanted to hear was that there was a party going on somewhere that he wasn't invited to, or worse still wouldn't have been allowed to go to anyway. All the same, he shrugged, it was so boring this life of doing the right thing. We stood there on the steps of St. Basil's Cathedral in Red Square, along with all the other out-of-towners and tourists, waiting to watch the changing of the guard at the gates of the Kremlin. I don't think either of us knew what difference any of it really made.

A couple of weeks later back in London I ran into him again, this time with Sharon. It was at the old Capital Radio building in Euston tower, where I was then presenting a weekly rock show. I was surprised to see them, as normally someone would have called ahead to let me know they were coming in. As soon as I started talking to them though, I realised something was wrong. Sharon, who despite the almost sickeningly cutesy demeanour she often adopts on TV shows these days, had never been clingy in the old-fashioned sense. But this afternoon she seemed to be hanging onto Ozzy for dear life, wrapped around him like a cloak. As soon as he started speaking, though, it became clear why. He was off his head. Not on booze or drugs – or not illegal drugs anyway – but something else. It was well known to me by then that since he'd begun his period clean-ups at Sharon's behest five years before that Ozzy had become a walking pharmacist's, permanently loaded up with bottles of pills of all descriptions. One day he had taken the trouble to talk me through some of them, pulling out bottles from every conceivable place: his jacket pockets, his carry-bag, tables and drawers and various cupboards. Along with the bundles of high-denomination notes he also habitually carried around with him – a hangover from his poverty-stricken past, he explained – he now carried enough bottles of pills to make him rattle – that is, if his various pieces of clunky, clinky jewellery weren't already making enough noise as it was. In short, I knew he was weird but this was definitely something different. He just didn't seem all there. Not in his usual semi-befuddled way. He seemed genuinely to have vanished inside himself somewhere. I noticed he was perspiring heavily too. He looked like a ghost in chains. One of those ghosts that carry around their head tucked under their arm.

Sharon hid whatever she was really feeling behind the smile and the charm as she always did when Ozzy was having one of his 'bad days'. They were off to Hamley's toy store, in Regent Street, she said, to buy their daughter Aimee a birthday present. 'My precious baby is going to be six,' Sharon grinned, holding tight to Ozzy's arm. They were having a little party for her that Saturday night.

I had asked Ozzy how he was enjoying being back at home again after Moscow. He shook his head and frowned. 'It's all right. I'm bored already, though. I don't know what to do with myself. Why don't you come up to the house for a drink sometime?' A drink? Was he off the wagon again then? I looked at Sharon but her face was still giving nothing away. 'Yes,' she said. 'Come up and keep the old man company. He's driving me mad wandering around the house with nothing to do.'

Then we parted; they had Hamley's to get to and I had a show to put together. But as I watched them leave I couldn't help but wonder what was wrong. I had seen Ozzy suffering from what might be termed post-tour syndrome before – that unsettling come-down period performers often go through when they first return home from a long world tour – but this seemed like something else. What, though, who knew? I expected Sharon would sort it out for him eventually, just like she always did. Then I forgot about it. Until...

That Sunday night I was at home watching *News at Ten* on the telly when an item came on that took me a few moments to take in. 'Rock star Ozzy Osbourne has been arrested...' the newsreader seemed to be saying. In that microsecond between him delivering the rest of the sentence and my brain kicking into gear I assumed he would say something about being drunk and disorderly or in possession of drugs, perhaps. Something rock star-ish like that anyway. Except it wasn't anything like that, it was something so completely unexpected I really couldn't quite believe it. He said: 'Osbourne, 40, was arrested in the early hours of Sunday morning after allegedly trying to strangle his wife and manager, Sharon Osbourne...'

'What did he say?' I asked my girlfriend, sitting on the couch next to me. 'What the fuck did he say?' Then the phone rang. It was a producer from Capital Radio calling to ask if I'd heard the news and whether I'd do a piece for their own eleven o'clock news bulletin. It still hadn't quite sunk in yet, though. *Ozzy* had been *arrested* for trying to...*strangle Sharon?* It wasn't real. It couldn't be. But I had only seen them a couple of days before. And then I remembered the vacant look in Ozzy's bulletproof eyes and I thought, 'Oh, shit...'

The next couple of days my phone didn't stop ringing. This was long before email and the only way for people to get in touch was by phone. Suddenly, it seemed, the whole world wanted to know me. Neither Ozzy nor Sharon was talking to the media so they were doing the next best thing and ringing round anyone and everyone that had ever known them that they could get a phone number for. As my book on Ozzy, *Diary Of A Madman*, had come out a couple of years before, my name seemed to be fairly near the top of everyone's list, from the *Sun*, the *Mail* and *The Times* to foreign publications like the *National Enquirer*, the *New York Post*, the *LA Times*, even things like *Paris Match* in France, *Der Bild* in Germany and various outposts of *Rolling Stone*, *Playboy*, and several others. Fortunately, answer machines had been invented and mine was in permanent employment until I could figure out what to do. After all, what did I know about what had happened? Just like everyone else, the first I'd heard of it was on the news...

The papers were full of it anyway, with or without any help from me. 'DEATH THREAT' OZZY SENT TO BOOZE CLINIC! screamed the headline in the *Sun*. BAN ON SEEING WIFE! cried the *Mirror*. HELL OF DRYING OUT! wailed the *Star*. According to the reports, the police had arrived at the house in the early hours of

Sunday morning and subsequently arrested Ozzy for trying to strangle Sharon, or 'intending her to fear that the threat would be carried out' as the official police report put it. They also trotted a slew of rumours which may or may not have had anything to do with anything: Ozzy was clinically insane; Sharon had been having an affair; Don had gotten to Ozzy and persuaded him to get rid of Sharon. It was a bizarre mixture of half-baked theories and utter codswallop. Typical tabloid fare, you might say, except when it concerns someone you actually know, extremely hard to swallow.

Then the phone rang again late one night and this time the voice leaving a message was Sharon's. I picked up. Understandably, she sounded washed-out, far from her usual no-problem self. For the first time since I'd first met her, in fact, she sounded vulnerable and afraid. Not so much she wasn't already starting to bounce back – hence the call – but you could tell she'd been through it.

'What had happened?' I asked, 'Had he finally just gone mad or what?'

'Yes,' said Sharon, 'I think he had. Because that wasn't the Ozzy I know, that was…someone else.'

I was surprised to even be speaking to her. I had assumed…'No, it's all right,' she said, 'We *want* to talk about it.'

Yes, it was true, Ozzy had turned nasty and attacked her, but he had been drunk, she said. Blind drunk. 'It was like he just blacked out – and someone else appeared.'

It was the case of Russian vodka the organisers of the Moscow shows had given him, she explained. He had been steadily working his way through a bottle over dinner that night when a niggling argument escalated into something 'completely out of control.' She sighed. 'We've had lots of fights before,' said Sharon, 'you know what we're like, but nothing like this. I knew I was in serious shit when he started talking as "we". As in, "We've decided you've got to go…" It wasn't Ozzy and that's what terrified me. Ozzy would never ever have done that to me or anyone, because he's just not capable of it. But when Ozzy gets loaded, Ozzy disappears and someone else takes over…'

The house had its own specially installed security system and the police were there within minutes of Sharon hitting the 'panic button'. Following his arrest, Ozzy spent the next 36 hours banged-up in a cell at Amersham police station, while he waited to appear before Beaconsfield Magistrates Court on the Monday morning. Inside the courtroom that day, she said, were over 50 reporters and photographers. After a brief hearing, Ozzy was placed on bail under three conditions: 1) That he immediately check into an alcoholic rehabilitation programme at a live-in centre of his choice. 2) That he make no attempt whatsoever to contact Sharon. 3) That he make no attempt to return to the family home until told to do so by the courts.

Ozzy was taken from the courthouse back to Amersham police station where he was met by his long-time personal assistant Tony Dennis, who drove him straight to Huntercombe Manor: a private, £250-a-day rehab joint in Buckinghamshire already familiar to the singer, who had been admitted there briefly for treatment twice already in the past year. Sharon told me that the doctors at Huntercombe that examined him decided it would be three months at least before Ozzy would be in a fit state to go home. She also said she had dropped the attempted murder charge as soon as Ozzy had agreed to go into rehab. 'Alcohol is destroying his life. To be an alcoholic means you have a disease. If Ozzy had cancer people would feel sorry for him. But because he's an alcoholic people don't understand. He just needs to get help.' To that end, she said, she had

182

decided to drop her charges against him, on the condition he stay put in rehab until he was properly well again. 'Whatever's wrong with Ozzy, it's not something that's going to take six weeks in a rest home to cure,' she said wearily. 'It's going to take a lot longer than that to get Ozzy well again. But no matter how long it takes, the children and I will be there waiting for him. I am not divorcing him. I just want him to get well…'

She invited me to visit him at the Manor. Again, I expressed surprise. Surely Ozzy was in no fit state to be interviewed? But Sharon was insistent. 'He's got a lot he wants to get off his chest. But he doesn't trust talking to anyone else from the press.' What could I say except yes? The thought of joining Ozzy in his rehab cell was hardly an appetising one but she sounded absolutely desperate and the last thing I wanted was to add to her woes. 'Well, if you're sure,' I said, 'and Ozzy's sure…' They were sure, she said. 'It will do him good.' What it would do for me was not discussed. I had never seen inside one of those places before and had no idea what to expect. I knew it wouldn't be a padded cell. Nevertheless, what did they look like, those gaffs? Like hospitals? Like prison cells? I supposed I was about to find out. I just hoped Humpty wasn't in too many pieces…

A few days later, Tony, Ozzy's long-suffering assistant, was driving me up a long, tree-lined, gravel-strewn path towards a large building in the style of the traditional English country manor, tucked away in its own private acreage. We arrived at about 7.30 on an already darkening Sunday evening, two weeks to the day since Ozzy's arrest. The lobby was part plush hotel reception, part gleaming dentist's waiting room. Sunday was one of the two days a week the patients were allowed visitors and various people milled about while I waited for Ozzy in the communal TV room. It was easy to separate the 'guests' from the 'visitors': the former were the ones sitting around looking relatively relaxed; the latter the ones shuffling self-consciously and snatching furtive glances at their watches.

Suddenly there he was, 'feeling nervous,' he said, and 'in need of a ciggy.' He had just finished another session with his therapist and 'me fuckin' head is still going.' He kept the chatter up all the way to his room on the first floor. Like a suite at some plush but gloomy provincial hotel, Ozzy's living quarters comprised one large bedroom-cum-living room, with en suite bathroom and toilet, plus another smaller sitting room. Well furnished but bland, I noticed there was also a phone and fax machine in the main room. No TV, though. 'They don't want you sat on your own in your room for too long,' he explained.

'It's a bit like a hotel,' I said, trying to sound encouraging.

'Yeah, except you can't go downstairs to the bar...'

Ozzy whipped out an ashtray from where he'd stashed it under the bed and lit a cigarette. 'It's against the rules to smoke in your room but fuck it,' he sighed, 'it's all I've got left...'

I placed the tape recorder on a coffee table strewn with packs of Marlboro, a pot of decaffeinated coffee, plus endless chocolate bars and half-finished cans of Diet Coke – a sweet tooth being a common sign of alcohol withdrawal, he told me forlornly. Despite everything, he didn't look too bad, actually. Not on the outside anyway. Dressed in matching black T-shirt and gym pants, he looked surprisingly trim, in fact. He pointed to the treadmill machine in the corner. 'I've been using that,' he said. 'It helps relieve the boredom...'

I had intended to broach the subject of how he came to be there, slowly. But sitting with him alone in his room, there was simply no other place to start. Did he remember attacking Sharon? 'I can only take what's been told to me, but I assume she's right because…I mean, it really shook my wife up. Really, what I suppose it's true to say happened, was we had a domestic argument that went a bit over the edge because I was pissed. Which happens every night of the week to some people, but when it happens to me everybody gets to hear about it. Everybody rows. I suppose I was pissed and I took it a little too far and threatened to kill her…But it's snowballed yet again, same as all the other incidents. It's just gone way out of proportion. I just wish everybody would back off. I'm very much still in love with my wife, you know? I don't wish anyone any harm. But just leave us alone.'

He said he had actually been sober for over four months prior to the two Moscow shows. Then someone had to give him that damned vodka. 'It was all right for about a week or so, on the vodka,' he said wistfully, 'then I became like a closet case – I started drinking and not telling anybody. Till in the end…apparently, Sharon and I were having a few words…I think she suspected…I mean, my paranoia stepped in, you know, and I just had an alcoholic blackout.'

Because of that, he said, he could remember very little of the actual incident which led to Sharon calling the cops. 'I became a blackout drinker about a year ago…as far as I know. I may have been one for many years and never realised it. [But] I vaguely remember going to a Chinese restaurant with Sharon [and the family]…just bits and pieces, you know…I'd drunk a bottle of vodka that day. Then I woke up in jail and all my face was scratched where Sharon had tried to defend herself. I didn't know what had happened. I could remember being nicked but I thought maybe I'd fallen over when they were dragging me out of the house. It was like a mad dream. Even in the police car, I thought, "This isn't real…"'

He had been in jail before, of course, but the two nights Ozzy spent at Amersham police station were 'the worst of my life. I just couldn't believe what they said I'd done.' Fortunately, the police had treated him kindly. 'I was in a cell on my own and they gave me cigarettes and chatted to me once in a while. Conditions were disgusting, though. I know they're not meant to be like Butlin's but they were terrible. Not fit for a rat...'

What really bothered him, he said, was the way the whole story had been played out in the press; from unsubstantiated rumours that Sharon had been having an affair and it was this that the couple had been arguing over that night, to rumours that Ozzy was intending to fire Sharon as his manager and go back to her father, Don Arden, thereby sparking a full-on Sabbath reformation. He shook his head wearily. 'They've built the whole thing way out of proportion. I'm *not* divorcing Sharon. I'm *not* rejoining Black Sabbath. I'm *not* going back to Don. I just wish everybody would back off and leave my family alone, you know? Leave us alone!'

He said that Sharon had since pledged to stand by him, and that he'd also received hundreds of letters of support from fans and well-wishers. Ultimately, he said, the pressure of touring 'just got to me and I blew up. That's what happens to me, I've got no other way of getting rid of the frustration. Other people go to the pub, have a few drinks and mellow out. I can't do that. I'm a chronic alcoholic and I'm in a chronic alcoholic phase.' He claimed he had even made an appointment to check into Huntercombe Manor the week before the incident. 'But my alcoholic mind was telling me, "Don't go Ozzy, pull out at the last minute and go up north to some drinking friends of yours and get smashed for a week". This was all planned in my sick head...'

Then he got arrested. 'I'm just glad I'm here now. I miss my kids, and my home, but I have a lot of hope now. A *lot* of hope. Because I don't want to go down the scale any further than that. That was pretty bad, what I did. But I've met people a lot worse off than me that have got well on this programme.' Did something drastic like that have to happen to make him sober up? 'Maybe so…Everybody I've met that's got sober said to me, "Ozzy, you're heading for a major calamity". But you haven't got a chance on the road. I was whacking cortisone in me twice a month just to keep going. And it's all mind-altering, it's all a drug.' Consequently, 'I was fucking crazy by the time I came off the last tour. Absolutely insane! I'm still not sane now. I'm still on medication in this place.'

What was the root cause of it all, though? Did he even know? He spoke of the rigours of touring but he was at home when he attacked Sharon. He shook his head, as though trying to stir up the dregs of his memory. Touring, he admitted, 'isn't all of it, no, but it's a big part of it.' It was 'the old Catch 22.' You toured to get the money to pay for the big house you never lived in – because you were always away touring. 'My kid starts to walk, my kid starts school, my kid takes part in school sports – I'm never there for any of it! I just get pissed off with it.' Then, when you did finally come home, 'that's an anti-climax, too. I think, when I get home I'm gonna take Jack [then only four] out on my bike. I'm gonna buy the girls [Aimee, six, and Kelly, five] a little paddling pool. I wanna do all those things that fathers are supposed to do. I think about how it's gonna be sunny, it's gonna be this, it's gonna be that. But when you get there it's never how you pictured it. It's either raining or they've run out of paddling pools or the bike's broken.' He lit another cigarette and blew out the smoke. 'I get bored so easily, too. I've just been seeing my therapist and he said,

187

"You've got to learn some relaxation". I said, I've never relaxed since the day I was born! I can't sit still for a moment.'

He paused and frowned. 'The truth is I don't understand why I get drunk. I don't understand any of it. My intention that morning wasn't...I mean, I didn't get up and think, "Oh, it's a great day to go to the pub, get smashed as a rat, come back, drink a bottle of vodka and strangle the wife". That was not my intention. I just wanted to have a few drinks and mellow out. But I go crazy with booze now.'

He said the children had been to see him that day for the first time since his arrest; an event that left them all in tears. 'Today, when my children left me, that was enough for me to want to stop. They were all crying, looking out the back of the Range Rover, and my heart broke. I thought, "What a fucking arsehole you are, Ozzy. What a total dickhead! You're saying goodbye to your kids again when you should be at home with them".' He stared at me. 'I beat myself up about it, I get really down...Being in a place like this, it's kind of lonely, you know?' His face fell and I thought he might start crying again. Then, recovering, he added jovially: 'You don't know if they're gonna put electrodes to your balls or what...'

What did they actually do for him there? 'It's like a therapy thing. You talk in a group to other alcoholics. I can't really give too much away because it's supposed to be anonymous but there's a lot of people here from all walks of life and we sit in a group and we discuss our problems and we recognise similarities. You always think you're the only one that does these crazy things. But you find out that everybody who's an alcoholic does exactly the same. There's a pattern to it and so you talk it out instead of bottling it up. I'd say something like, "whenever I have the third drink I go a bit funny in the head" and the guy in charge will ask if anyone else relates to that and someone will say they can. So it makes you feel a little bit more at ease with yourself. I'm not gonna try any of these aversion therapies though, where you take this pill, have eight bottles of vodka and throw up. I used to do that without taking a pill...'

He complained that Sharon – who had over recent years moved on in her own career to manage several other high-profile eighties acts such as the Quireboys and Lita Ford – 'never stops working, which kind of gets on my tits sometimes. Because when I come off tour I wanna be with my wife and family, and she's still a manager for other bands. I get pretty resentful over it. Then I get bored. But I've got to work it out somehow or other. I still love her very, very much.'

I asked what sort of medication he was on. 'Antidepressants, mostly. Because the side-effects of the cortisone make you very depressed, you think the whole world's coming down on your shoulders. And I'm on various anti-fit pills because I became a fit-drinker, a spasm drinker.' He explained how when withdrawing from alcohol once before he had gone into a spasm because he 'didn't have a medical detox.' He went on: 'This was about six months ago. It's not as bad as it sounds, but if you've got a record of having these seizures they keep you on this medication. I'm on all kinds of different medication.'

And how long was he planning on staying there? 'As long as it takes. I've got to get well this time because it could have been worse: I could have ended up killing my wife. The usual thing is four to six weeks, but I'm not even thinking about that. I'm thinking about three to six months, maybe even longer. There's no time limit. My wife's still in shock, my kids...We're all still in shock over this episode, because it wasn't me in my full...' He struggled to find the words. 'I didn't mean to...in my wildest dreams I wouldn't have wanted to...do that.'

His 'number one priority right now,' said Ozzy, was 'to get sober and stay sober. I know I've got to go to constant therapy classes for the rest of my life. I've got to go to [AA] meetings…I've got to meet up with other recovering alcoholics. Two recovering alcoholics can do more for each other than any psychiatrist or therapy. Ultimately, I've got two choices: either get it right this time or screw up again. And if I don't get it right, I'll either die or go insane…'

I asked him if there was any truth whatsoever in the newspaper stories that Don had been in touch with him again and to my surprise he said that both Don and Sharon's brother David had tried to get in contact with him, even going so far as to send him faxes to his room at Huntercombe. He got up and showed me one in which Don referred to Sharon as 'that witch' and basically offered to take over things for him in the event that Sharon decided to make good on her threat to divorce him or proceed with her court action. 'They even tried to call me in the jail,' Ozzy said. 'I got telegrams and all that. I mean, I appreciate the thought, but I think they need to take care of their own business and leave me alone. Me and my family are doing okay as we are. I don't need their help. I'm a big boy now. I'm not the vegetable that they used to call me any more.'

The most important thing now, he said, was that 'Sharon and I are still together. That we're all back to normal, and I can learn a bit more tolerance. And that we have happy days for the rest of our lives, you know? I can't speak for Sharon because I've learnt in this place not to speak for anybody else any more. I presume, at the end of the day, she wants to settle down, though.'

This, it seemed to me, was the saddest part of all. On paper, he should be the happiest man in the world. 'Instead, you end up in a rehab joint on an attempted murder charge,' he said. 'Happiness doesn't come from high finance, though. It helps a great deal. I mean, people say, I'd rather be wealthy and unhappy than poor and unhappy. And I'm not going to give it to some far-off fucking charities, you can forget that! But it's like, what's the point in working if you don't appreciate what you're working for?'

Had he actually tried meditation or any other relaxation techniques? 'Well, part of the therapy is a kind of a meditation exercise. When I say "meditation" people out there will probably think I'm talking about the guru and all that. But it's nothing like sitting there going, OOMMMM! We just shout PINTS!' He laughs. 'PINTS! And BROWN AALLLEEEE!!! No, it's all right. I feel safe here, you know? It's when I'm out there…I walk out the house, in the yard, in my studio, out of my studio, in my yard, back in the house. I'm like a bloody praying mantis! Yet when I'm on the road for long periods of time it's worse. I've been on the road for over 20 years, you know? And I really don't enjoy being out on the road for huge long periods of time. It would be worth it if I could go home every two weeks or something. But it don't work like that.

'At this point, Mick, my number one priority is to get sober and stay sober. I never again want to be in a bar. I've said this a million times before, I know, and always ended up in a bar. But I have hope that I can kick this booze thing and get straight once and for all. It's like a love affair I have with booze. It's like, you know it's killing you but you can't stop. It's like any addiction. You know it's killing you but you just can't put the stuff down. No alcoholic person out there goes, "Oh shit yeah, I got pissed for a week, I don't wanna talk about it". I mean, Sharon used to drink a lot of booze many years ago. But she got up one morning we were in Monmouth, and she said, "Fucking hell, Ozzy, I feel like shit,

I'm never gonna drink again". And she's never drunk since, as far as I know.'

They say that a lot of alcoholics are actually allergic to alcohol, and that's what makes it so addictive. The body becomes addicted to the poison and the rest is all a major allergic reaction. 'I heard that before, yeah. Maybe I am, I don't know. All I know is, I am an alcoholic and my name is Ozzy. And I've got to take certain steps to try and arrest the disease. Because I'm either gonna kill myself, kill someone else, which I very nearly did, or I'm gonna go insane, I'm gonna be locked away in an insane asylum. It's got to that point now where I don't get happy-pissed, I go bulldozing around. I don't even know what I'm doing or where I'm at. Sharon says she's terrified when she sees me drink now. It upsets the whole family, close friends and everybody that works for me. You should do an article on some of the people who have been around me the last 12 months. I've been like Dr Jekyll and Mr Hyde, you know? And I'm really like that when I get drunk – from Dr Jekyll to Mr Hyde, every time. But I can't keep saying, I'm "cured", mate – you know, cured in inverted commas – because I never will be cured from it. I accept that now. I've just got to take certain steps. I've got to be on medication for a while because I became a manic depressive from the cortisone shots. I mean, major depressions. But if I can just reaffirm, I'm in treatment. But there's no guard outside the door. I'm not in shackles. I'm not getting electrodes round my bollocks…'

I remarked that it was nice to see he'd been able to keep some of his sense of humour about this. 'All in all, that's about the only thing I have got, which cheers not only me up but all the rest of the people here. We have a scream here. Somehow it's easy to laugh at your troubles. Yet I can have double-platinum records and all the rest of the shit and I'm still unhappy about it. I'll always find a fucking fault in anything. That's the artistic temperament, I suppose.'

What was the main reason he had asked me here this evening, though? What was it he wanted to tell the world the most? 'I just wanted to set the record straight. I picked up the newspaper and I read "Ozzy gets divorced", and it's not that at all! I mean, not as far as I'm aware of. Sharon was round this afternoon. I asked her then, "Are you going to divorce me?" She said, "Absolutely not". And I want to say that I'm not gonna let people from the outside fuck my marriage up. Nobody thought we would last as long as we have, but we have. And I hope to God that we last as long as the rest of our lives.'

If the worst came to the worst, though, and they did split up, would he go back on the bottle? 'The very worst thing that could happen to me would be if me and Sharon were to split up. But if it did happen, I wouldn't drink, no. I can't drink. Because that would fuck everything up even more. And that's what I've gotta say to myself – no matter what, I don't pick up that first drink. There's no such thing for me any more as just-have-a-half-Ozzy. One's too many and ten's not enough for me. Once I'm off I'll drink the fucking planet dry! And when you hear of people like Phil Lynott dying, or John Bonham and all that, you think: that will never happen to me. But it fucking will. It's catching up with me rapidly. I don't wanna be the next fucking victim, you know?'

He went on: 'I've always been a paranoid person. Always. Ultra-paranoid. I'm very nervous and shy, too. When I'm performing, that's a different person again. The performing Ozzy is nothing like the person you see now. At least, I fucking hope not. I mean, I don't suppose Laurel and Hardy walked around in the silly hats when they were offstage, and neither do I. But some people look at me and they expect me to walk around with a fucking bag full of bats! "Hi there, wanna bat?" It's not real, you know? It's called entertainment.'

Before we turned off the tape he mentioned that Sabbath guitarist Tony Iommi had also phoned him while he'd been in rehab. 'I wouldn't pick up his call, though. I haven't spoken to the fucking dickhead since Live Aid and even then he didn't say goodbye. So what's he suddenly become my old pal for? I mean, I'm not that much of a dickhead that I can't see that. I'm stoned, I'm not fucking brain-dead! Not yet, anyway, old bean. Not yet...'

A few days later I met up with Sharon in London for lunch. She was as immaculately turned out as always but if you looked closely you could see the worry still in her eyes, hear the weariness in her voice. But at least her smile was back, and her sense of humour. I noticed, though, that she barely ate a thing, just some soup and some water.

'How did he look to you?' she asked.

'Better than I thought he would,' I replied. 'Frightened by himself, by what he'd done.'

'Good,' she said. 'I want him to realise what he's done. Not to punish him but just to try and make him want to stop, or at least do something about it. The thing is, I know that wasn't him trying to kill me that night. Ozzy is the sweetest guy in the world, he really wouldn't harm a fly. But he's got a disease called alcoholism and it's killing him.'

She talked of the times before when she had come so close to walking out on him for good. How behind all the laughs they always had together there were so many tears she didn't know how she had coped sometimes. 'I was out the fucking door more than once, I can tell you,' she said. 'I'd have the three kids packed and ready to go and then I would think, but where will we go, what will we do? Then Ozzy would sober up for a while and things would be wonderful again. Until the next time...'

She went on: 'He'd be off his head on tour and you'd think, "Oh well, he'll be better when we get him home". Then he'd come home and there'd be nothing for him to do and he'd start drinking even more. Some mornings he'd be off down the pub before it even opened. We bought a house once that had a pub at the bottom of the drive. Big fucking mistake! He used to joke and say we should have bought the pub instead cos he spent more time there. I used to think it was funny, the way he would act after a few drinks. And it was funny for a while, the funny voices and the stupid stories, it was all very playful. But it's got worse and he's not like that any more when he drinks. He turns into...someone else. And I don't like that person. I want my real Ozzy back.'

I told her I hoped he'd be back soon. In truth, though, I wasn't hopeful. Free at last from Don, more successful than ever even without Sabbath, the parents of three beautiful children, these should have been the best years of Sharon's and Ozzy's lives. Instead, I had never seen them so distraught, so fearful of the future. Exactly a decade on from Sharon first taking Ozzy under her wing, steering him through the eighties, you wondered what on earth the nineties would have in store for them.

Act 11
Scene Six:

Any Colour You Like as Long as it's Black

'I went to see *Spinal Tap* and I didn't think it was funny,' said Ozzy, chuffing on a large cigar and allowing the smoke to gather in contemplative clouds about his head. 'I thought it was a fucking documentary, I did. When they got lost on their way to the stage, that happened to me a thousand times! Some cunt didn't change the signs around and you'd end up in the fucking car park with your guitar and your fucking platforms on in the rain...'

We were sitting in his 'play room' (snooker table, air-guns, studio-size hi-fi) in the same huge mansion in Buckinghamshire in which he'd tried to strangle Sharon eight years before. I remarked that he'd come a long way since then.

'Yes and no,' he said. 'I might not be trying to kill anybody but I'm still fucking insecure, I'm still crazy. I still think I'm going to fail at everything I do. I think that's in my make-up. I'm still taking Prozac.'

Nevertheless, a lot of demons had been put to rest over that period.

ANY COLOUR YOU LIKE AS LONG AS IT'S BLACK

Ozzy may have been back on his 'pity pot' again drinking and doing drugs by the time he and I were spending time together in LA in the early nineties, but it had been a steady crawl up from the bottom of the well ever since.

'I had to,' he said. 'I was in my forties and just couldn't take the hangovers any more. Plus it was fucking everything up. It's like Sharon said, it just wasn't funny any more. People talk about the success, and there's no doubt, I've been lucky, but there were so many other things I got wrong too.'

I asked him for some examples. 'One of the reasons why I never concentrated on Europe was because [Sharon] took me to Germany when I was permanently pissed and I fucked it up. Sharon says, "Listen, we've got to make a good impression with these fuckers and you can't be doing it or we're never gonna get nowhere". Anyway, to cut a long story short…one of the people at CBS Germany invited me to dinner thinking I was fucking Donny Osmond or something. So this fucking drunken fuck-pig walks into his restaurant and he goes, "Vass is diss?" And there was this huge table and there were these two contest winners from America that won a contest to fly all the way to Germany to spend the evening with Ozzy Osbourne. And I mean, I was *legless*, fucking legless! And when you're drunk in a restaurant and it's all formal, you can't wait to get the grub down you except it takes fucking hours for them to serve it. So I got bored, I got up, drunk a bottle of wine down, took all my clothes off, walked across the table, sat in front of this big, burly German with his beard, put my legs around him on the table, and given him a big kiss in this big beard. And Sharon's going, "Oh, my God!" Within 10 minutes, the entire of the hot-line of CBS was notified: this man is never allowed in my country again! I will destroy him if he comes! That's

197

why we never got any records punted in Europe, because of that. It took 'em years for them to forgive me for that. Sharon was on the plane coming back going, "You can fucking stick this…" Tearing up all the contracts on the plane. A wild fucking time, that was. But at that point, I was crazy. I was just thinking, "Oh, here we go. Move over Keith Moon, I'm next", you know?'

Did he ever seriously believe he would end up killing himself? 'Oh, every other day! Every other day…'

'What stopped you – Sharon?'

'Absolutely without any shadow of a doubt in my mind, I wouldn't be sitting here now, without any shadow of a doubt. I mean, she…she…she had the patience of a saint. I mean, Mick, you saw me in my fucking glory days. I mean, there's a funny side of it, but there's also a very sad side of it, too. I don't know whether you ever had this, like as the day goes on it starts to come back to you and you go, "Oh, fuck! No! I didn't do that, did I? No!" It's like someone hitting you on the head with stones. And the next morning Sharon would go, "You've got to phone this one, this one and this one, apologise to that one, and beg this one for forgiveness." And I'd go why and she'd go, "Just fucking do it." Then as I was talking to them, it would come back to me and I'd just wanna go. If I knew what I was apologising for I would never have called, because I was so embarrassed. And then my worst nightmare that I always feared happened. I feared going into a drunken and drugged blackout and doing something without knowing I'm doing it. And that's when I got into trouble with Sharon.'

He paused, took a big chuff on his cigar. 'Then again, it didn't stop me drinking. But that was the beginning of the end because I would drink and I would just get to a point…See, at the end of my drinking, I would drink so much and then I would want coke. I mean, to keep

me going all night. And then Sharon turned round to me one day –
we'd had the babies by that time – and she said, "If you *ever* come in
this house with cocaine again, I'll call the police and have you
arrested." And I said, okay, no more, it'll never happen again.'

He said he didn't 'keep count' but when I asked Sharon she
confirmed that Ozzy had been straight – 'more or less' – for over three
years now. 'I mean, I've dabbled and I've smoked a joint here and
there,' he said, 'I've had a fucking Valium here and there and
whatever. But the way I look at it, in the old days I used to wake up
lying in my own urine and puke every morning, every single morning.
And you'd think that after so much of that a normal person would go,
"Why am I fucking doing this? Look at me, I'm lying in this shit and
puke and piss and whatever." Normal, rational people would go, "I'm
not a fucking animal." But I'd get in the shower and when I put clean
clothes on I felt new again.'

We sat there holding onto our cigars, remembering…

The early nineties had been a rocky time. Sharon had decided the
best way to keep her sanity – short of divorcing the bastard – was to
try her hand at managing other acts as well as Ozzy. She had
considerable success too, almost a Midas touch. The first artist she got
involved with had been Lita Ford. Lita had been the guitarist in the
original all-girl rock band, The Runaways. Their singer Joan Jett had
gone on to solo stardom but despite several albums Lita had never had
a sniff. The fact that Don had also managed Lita briefly was probably
a spur, too, Sharon admitted, but the fact is she went all out for Lita
– rebuilding her image, bringing in songwriters to help her out – and
the result was the one and only hit album of her career, *Lita*. Ozzy was
jealous but was in no position to say anything as Sharon had also
managed the singular feat of pairing him and Lita together for a duet

on an Ozzy song called 'Close My Eyes For Ever', which went on to become the biggest single he or Lita ever had, a giant hit all over the world. So far, so Ozzy shut your mouth...

Sharon got into hotter water with him though over her next two signings: a London-based band called the Quireboys, who again Sharon took from the clubs and shit-holes of London to the biggest stages in the world, helping them produce a debut album, *A Bit Of What You Fancy*, which was Top Five in every major market in the world, bar the US. Finally, she signed Bonham – the band belonging to Jason Bonham, the son of the late Led Zeppelin drummer John Bonham, and a fantastic drummer in his own right. Bonham were like the opposite of the Quireboys, in that their album, *A Disregard of Timekeeping*, was a big hit in America, and nowhere else. Suddenly, Sharon was a hot manager no one in the biz could accuse any longer of merely having married into her success – an old and hugely unfair accusation she still nonetheless suffered from in the male-oriented, dick-first rock biz. Suddenly more and more artists wanted to secure her services – Lemmy's Motorhead were said to be in the frame as were several others – and she began entertaining the idea of fronting her own Los Angeles-based management organisation.

None of which made Ozzy happy at all. He understood, he said, that Sharon needed to 'do her own thing,' but he didn't like the idea of her spending so much time away with other (male) bands, particularly the Quireboys, who had a – justifiable – reputation for drugging and boozing almost as lurid as his own. Hence, our bizarre late-night conversation in 1991 which led to him calling Sharon on the phone to tell her he didn't want her managing him any more. As it turned out, this was a complaint Sharon had grown used to hearing. She told me: 'It's his paranoia, it sends him nuts sometimes thinking

I'm out there working with other people. Yet he knows there will never be anyone more important to me than him, not just as an artist but as my husband and the father of our children. But you try telling him that once he's got a bee in his bonnet...'

As an example, she cited the Christmas party she had had at the house in Buckinghamshire one year, to which everyone she worked with had been invited – except Ozzy. 'He was away touring at the time, and I wanted the children to have something to enjoy,' she shrugged. I had also been at the party and later made the mistake of telling Ozzy how great it had been and how much everyone had enjoyed it. 'Oh, great, you too,' he grimaced. Why, what was wrong? 'Do you know how much that party I never even knew about cost me?' he barked. 'Thirty grand! How would you like it if your old lady went and spent thirty grand of your money on a fucking party you weren't even invited to?' I had to admit, it didn't sound too enticing a prospect. But when I told Sharon what Ozzy had said she exploded: 'It wasn't his fucking money, it was mine! That was the whole point. For the first time, I was making money of my own and I wanted to do something nice for the children. It's a shame he wasn't there but all he'd have done was get pissed anyway...'

Oh, dear. I decided to drop the subject. It had been a wonderful party, though...

The early nineties had also seen Ozzy announcing his retirement. I recalled talking on the phone to Sharon about it. 'He just can't handle it any more,' she told me matter-of-factly. 'He'll still make albums, still be involved in the business somewhere, but his days of living out of a suitcase are over.'

That had been in 1992, the year he officially bowed out in November that year with two shows in Costa Mesa, California, that had culminated with the other original members of Sabbath joining him on stage for the encores. What Sharon hadn't confided in me until a couple of years later, however, was that Ozzy had been diagnosed as suffering from multiple sclerosis. 'That's what some fucking asshole doctor in LA told us,' she said, 'and of course we believed him! Ozzy had had the shakes for years, you know that, but suddenly he developed a limp and so I sent him for a check up, the next thing they're doing blood tests and brain scans and they're telling us he's in the early stages of MS. I nearly fucking died when they told us.'

Indeed, it was months before a second and third opinion contradicted the first and Ozzy was given the all-clear. In the meantime, he had discussed his will and co-written a new song called 'See You on the Other Side' (which later appeared in his 1995 album, *Ozzmosis*). 'That's what that song is about,' said Sharon. 'We really thought he only had a few years left to live. So what with trying to keep him off the booze and drugs as well, we decided he shouldn't tour any more. Hence, the whole retirement thing…'

As Ozzy later revealed in an interview with the writer Philip Wilding, it wasn't until they were fairly sure he didn't have the disease after all that Ozzy even knew what the doctors had told Sharon. 'Unbeknown to me, the neurologist said to my wife: "I believe he has a little bit of multiple sclerosis". So she says to me: "I think you should retire". So, you know, she's in charge, she hasn't told me anything about me having this thing, and I'm like, okay, whatever you want. And I'm still on tour at the time, and I'm wearing this Swedish knee brace, and I've got atrophy in the leg because I wasn't using the muscle. Anyway, we get to New York, and every day Sharon's always crying. And I'm like: "What the fuck are you always crying for? What's up with you? Stop slurping around me".' He laughed. 'Of course, I still know nothing about this; I'm just taking handfuls of different pills and morphine shots, and I'm just this grinning fool around the place, pretending to be in pain when I wasn't so that the supply wouldn't dry up.'

When the truth finally came out, it was too late to stop the 'retirement' tour. Besides, by then Ozzy had almost convinced himself it was a good thing. 'She'd kept it from me, you know. But I'd announced the retirement, so I took a year off. Weird, isn't it? I'd retired because everyone thought I was dying of MS. Sharon said we can't let anyone know…and it turned out to be absolute bullshit. Terrible, now I think about it, the way I spoke to her – "Why are you slurping around me? Stop crying. Give me another bottle of those pain pills"…'

By the mid-nineties, Ozzy was back – headlining his own specially convened travelling outdoor festival, Ozzfest – and bigger, more successful than ever. Sharon, it seemed had done it again. Having steered Ozzy through the minefield of eighties rock – from the backcombed blond hair and glittery, shoulder-padded stage clothes of the Mötley Crüe era through the more downbeat, dark-haired jeans-and-T-shirt late eighties look and sound of groups like Metallica, right up to proto-nineties newbies like Marilyn Manson, which saw Ozzy affecting a similar zombie-like demeanour, a pair of blue-tinted 'granny glasses' perched nonchalantly on his nose – Ozzfest was by far her greatest coup yet. Laughed out of the room by the self-absorbed organisers of Lollapalooza – the American rock festival de jour of the early nineties – Sharon vowed to get her own back.

'They actually fucking laughed at the idea of Ozzy being on the Lollapalooza bill,' she told me, still spitting fury, 'They said he wasn't cool enough, these fucking little wankers who hadn't been born when

Ozzy was inventing heavy metal with Black Sabbath. So I thought, fuck them! We'll do our own festival…'

The result – Ozzfest, a travelling festival show headlined by Ozzy but featuring dozens of the newest, hottest bands across several stages, as well as secondary features such as 'chill out' zones, 'tattoo and piercing parlours' and all sorts of sidebar stalls dealing in everything from New Age paraphernalia to herbal remedies and hotdogs – became so successful so quickly that by its second year it had totally eclipsed Lollapalooza to become the largest dollar-grossing show of the American rock calendar, leaving Lollapalooza in the dust and – ironies of ironies – now considered so uncool it was called into abeyance not long after.

'I was so fucking pleased,' said Sharon. 'I thought: take that, you little cunts! Calling my husband uncool! Who's fucking uncool now?' she cackled.

You had to admire her. Having worked with every top manager and power broker in the American and British music biz over the past 30 years, the fact is I had never known one – not one – that came even close to matching Sharon Osbourne's astounding achievements. But she still had one more trick up her billowing sleeve, it seemed: thinking the unthinkable and actually getting Ozzy back with the original members of Black Sabbath again. Not just for one night either but an entire tour, maybe even an album and DVD too. 'Why not?' she shrugged when I expressed surprise, 'I've never been one to hold grudges – or not for long anyway,' she smiled sweetly. 'And anyway, Tony and the rest of the band are so much older now – we all are. Things have changed, and for the better.'

Ozzy and Sabbath had begun making their comeback with the Ozzfest tour of America in the summer of 1997. Then, in November that year, they headlined their first UK dates for nearly 20 years with a brace of shows at the NEC in Birmingham. Inevitably, the comeback shows got huge publicity. In America, it once again made Ozzfest the biggest dollar-grossing outdoor rock show of the year, while in Britain it signified the beginning of a new era in the biz: the arrival of the hugely profitable 'classic rock' market. Still, I said, sitting with Ozzy in his play room just a few weeks before the NEC shows, it must be weird being back together after all this time and so much water under the bridge…?

'Oh, God, it was like a whole war, yeah. I mean, I don't buy all this shit about, you know, I'll get fired but I'll still be friends. If you're still friends why get fired in the first fucking place? But it's so long ago now, it's like 20 fucking years ago, you know? And if anything that was the best kick up the arse I ever had in my career, because once I *knew* I could do it on my own, once I knew I didn't have to lean on them and listen to them, I was a free bird, and I could have fun with it.'

He became thoughtful again. 'You know what I've learnt, though? Never say never because, you know, time is a great healer. I mean, the amount of times I've seen you over the years and thought – is *that* Mick Wall? Suddenly you disappear for two fucking years and I find you've gone to sitting in a tree in the Himalayas and found a new method of getting yourself back to normal. It happens to us all, you know? It's like, you grow up. It's part of life. I mean, I suddenly got to a point in my life saying "If I go through my life *hating* someone, it's too time consuming". Hating someone or hating something, you've gotta sit there and spend as much time hating someone as you do liking someone, but it's in the negative end of the thing. It kind of eats you away inside. So if I dislike something a lot now, I just don't think about it. But to say "I hate you"…It's like the axe falls. There's nothing more you can say after "I hate you." I'd rather tell someone I love 'em. The three questions throughout my career were always: a) did you really bite the head off a bat? Then: did you piss up The Alamo? And, will we ever see you with Sabbath again? And I used to say, yes, yes, no. But, you know, Sharon's very, very clever, she makes you think it's your idea. I was like, "No! No! No! No!" But Sharon says "Give it a shot, see what you think". And you think, well, she's very good, and she's never steered me wrong yet…'

In fact, Sharon had been extremely shrewd – as ever – in her dealings with Black Sabbath. A couple of years before she had phoned to tell me she had now acquired legal rights to the name Black Sabbath after helping Tony Iommi – then the only original member still playing around the world under the Sabbath moniker – out of an embarrassing financial fix which found him briefly incarcerated in a Texan jail after his credit cards had been snipped, sending her own private plane – and lawyer – down to rescue him in return for his signing over the remaining rights to the Sabbath name. At the time she had wanted his plight known to the world as payback for all the years of grief he had delivered to both her and, most especially, Ozzy. Now the mood had changed. The upshot, all these years down the line, however, was that while she and Ozzy were prepared to forgive if not entirely forget what had gone on between them and Sabbath in the past, Ozzy and Sharon now held the whip hand when it came to deciding how and when and even *if* the group should proceed in the future.

'Ozzy was pushed around for years,' she said simply. 'I've made sure that never happens again.' Indeed she had.

So was this the happy ending then that she and Ozzy had longed for all this time? Sabbath and Ozzy reconciled, albeit with Sharon calling the shots, or was there still more to come, something she had planned that she hadn't told us – or even Ozzy – about yet?

She treated me to that wonderful, cheeky, told-you-so smile. 'Oh, I don't know,' she said. 'All I can say is if there's one thing I've learned over the years is that you're never dead in this business. So many times my old man was supposed to be on the way out the door but here we are, still doing well, still full of surprises. Who knows what might be round the corner?'

Before I left that day, Ozzy took me for a tour of the house. God knows why, I hadn't asked for one. Here was the kitchen – large, comfy, full of dogs and children – and here was the main lounge – huge and comfy, full of flowers and paintings and thick carpets, an enormous TV and yet more dogs and children. He even took me up to his and Sharon's bedroom, with its separate room for all Sharon's clothes and his own not inconsiderable wardrobe. Then his exercise room replete with bike, rowers, another big TV and endless Beatles' CDs. I said I felt like I was inside an episode of *Lifestyles of the Rich and Famous* and he just looked at me and grunted. 'Actually, we did one of them recently...' Yes, I had seen it. It was hilarious: Ozzy sticking the head of his pet parrot in his mouth as if to bite its head off, Sharon presiding over the almost gothic kingdom of their palatial Hollywood abode like the Queen of Sheba. The pair of them had been like a double-act and it reminded me of how funny they always were together whenever you went out with them for dinner or whatever.

'You should forget music and just be on TV,' I joked.

Sharon, who had just walked into the room, laughed and said, 'Do you know, that's exactly what someone else said after seeing that programme. We have thought about it. The trouble is, what would we do? Ozzy's hilarious but it's not like he's a joke teller or anything, and who wants to see me?'

'Maybe something like a chat show?' I ventured.

'Naw,' she shook her head. 'Ozzy would be more interesting than the guests.'

It was true. Ozzy on telly *would* be funny; so would Sharon. But what sort of programme could you put them in? Nothing anyone could think of. Not then, anyway...

Act III

In Which the Prince Of Darkness and the Good
Lady Sharon Will Live Happily Ever After – Even if
It Kills Them. Yes, It's Gone With the Wind
For the MTV Generation!

Scene One:

Mr Big Guns

I was standing on the platform waiting for the train home late one winter's night when my mobile rang. It was cold and late and raining and the trains were all fucked – again – and I had the horrible feeling that I might have to walk home if I wasn't careful. The phone ringing didn't help. Too miserable to care who it was I almost didn't answer. But when I gave it a glance it said: INTERNATIONAL CALL and curiosity got the better of me – again. I hit the button on the very last ring. It was Sharon calling from sunny LA.

'Hello, darling!' she trilled. I wondered what she wanted, Sharon never calling unless it is specifically about something. A new Ozzy album, perhaps, or some new band she wanted me to help her find a magazine cover for. The last thing I would have guessed it was about was…

'My father,' she said cheerily, 'Do you remember him?'

'What Don, you mean?' I asked incredulously. Of course I remembered him. Was he dead?

She laughed like champagne fizzing, 'No, nothing like that. He wants to do his memoirs. And he needs a writer to help, and I've recommended you. What do you think, my darling?'

I thought she must be taking the piss. 'Your *father*?' I repeated. 'But...'

'I know what you're thinking,' she said, 'but it's all okay now, we've made up.'

What?

'Yes, I know, I couldn't believe it either at first, but he's old now, he's changed.' She started burbling about 9/11 and how she and Ozzy had been in New York the day the twin towers came down and how it had 'changed everything, really altered our perspective.' I still didn't quite see what that had to do with the father she had barely spoken to for 20 years; the one she hated so much she had told her own children was dead, but then it's hard to think when you're talking on a mobile on the rain-swept platform of a train station to someone sitting by a swimming pool a thousand miles and several million dollars away. 'What do you think?' she said.

I didn't know what to think, other than to say yes, as you always did for Sharon. Besides, the thought of working with Don Arden on his memoirs, now there was a story I'd love to tell. Sharon told me she'd get her brother David to give me a ring the next day to make arrangements. David, who'd stuck by their father all these years, was still there then, holding the old man's hand, doing his bidding, right or wrong or in between. I still had to wait for my train home but the thought of meeting Don and talking to him about his life certainly made the time pass quicker.

Sure enough, David called the next day and explained the situation. He was the one that had instigated the Great Reconciliation. He confirmed that Sharon had been in a very different state of mind following the events of 9/11, but there was one other factor involved too: the old man was in the early stages of Alzheimer's. No longer a threat to anyone, David said, when he had broken the news to Sharon she had finally agreed to at least meet with their father, and see how it went.

'Then the moment she walked in the room and saw him it all just melted away,' said David, 'all the years of bitterness and recrimination, all the hatred, they just sat there together crying.'

Blimey. Now Sharon wanted to do something for her father, he said, before it was too late. Don had been working on the idea of his memoirs for several years, now he finally wanted to get them done and published. Could I help? Yes, of course I could. I rang my agent, Robert, as soon as I put the phone down from David, and set up a meeting for us all. First though, David said, I would have to come and meet Don myself – alone – to see how we got on. 'All…right,' I said. A time – one evening later that week – and a place – a pub round the corner from Park Lane, where the old man had rented an apartment while he was in London. I put the phone down looking forward to it. Then it rang again and it was my old friend Lynn, the one who had introduced me to Sharon so long ago. I hadn't spoken to her for a while and it was good to hear her voice again. Except it sounded strange, not unhappy just…under pressure. She came straight to the point. 'You're meeting Don, aren't you? I just wanted to warn you – be careful, that's all.'

But Sharon and David had said he was an old man, no threat to anyone any more, in the early stages of…

'I know all that,' said Lynn, 'But just be careful is all I'm saying. Don't trust him. Believe me, I know what I'm talking about. I've seen what he's done to Sharon over the years and it's not funny. He's got these eyes that just…' You could virtually hear the shudder down the phone. '…look straight through you.'

Don't worry, I said, trying to sound cheerful, I'll be careful. Anyway David would be there, I was sure I'd be all right. 'Mmm,' said Lynn. 'I hope so.'

As it turned out, they were all telling the truth, even if they were all only partially right. Don was old and clearly ailing, right as rain one minute, lapsing into the same story over again the next, and yes, he certainly did have the stillest, coldest eyes I've ever seen in anyone not yet dead. But he could also be painfully funny, and over the next nine months or so of working together I certainly enjoyed my time with him. It wasn't every day, after all, that one got to hang out with a genuine Mafiosi-connected throwback to the time when the music biz really did resemble the Wild West.

He was, however, still quite frightening when he wanted to be. He no longer actively hung people out of windows or placed loaded guns against their heads. But he was always quick to suggest that he still knew people that did. Once, when I was griping about certain people in the publishing world whom I was then momentarily disenchanted with (a normal conversation for most writers) he touched my arm and said, quite calmly, 'Do you want me to make some calls, kid? Get these fuckers sorted out for you?' I hurriedly shook my head, 'No, thanks, Don.' He looked at me, disappointed. 'Nice of you to offer, though,' I added. Those eyes again, 'Well, if you change your mind…'

How much of this was simple bravado and how much real, I'll never know. I sensed it was probably the former, but not enough to put it to the test. Not when he was continually telling me stories of all the different people he had 'sorted out' over the 50 years he had been in the business, or – even more chilling – the ones he'd still like to. He had never forgotten the broadcaster Roger Cook, for instance, who had submitted Don to one of his trademark door-stopping performances back in 1979, in the days when he presented a BBC Radio Four programme called *Checkpoint* (a precursor for his later TV series, *The Cook Report*). I remembered hearing that one and laughing out loud listening to Don telling Cook nonchalantly, 'Remember Mr Cook, legs do break, and I know where you live…' In my memory he had sounded positively blasé about the rotund reporter's needle-sharp questioning. Nearly a quarter of a century later, however, he swore to me that if he ever had 'the good fortune' to run into Cook 'in a pub or a restaurant perhaps or just out on the street' he would 'take him and kill him and I wouldn't care who was watching. I would kill him and I would do it slowly…'

Even when the memories were painful for him he never really flinched. For example, that watershed moment in the eighties when he so nearly ended up behind bars, only to see his beloved son David take the rap for him instead. Having decided that one of his accountants in LA had been siphoning off cash from his various businesses, Don went wild and had him abducted and brought to his home in England, where Don, as he freely admitted to me, had the man beaten, tortured and held prisoner. The result was an Old Bailey court case that effectively finished Don off. While he was miraculously cleared on charges of assault, kidnapping, blackmail and torture, David had been sentenced to two years' imprisonment for his part in proceedings. 'It broke my fucking heart,' Don told me, 'because David was always the good guy and had nothing to do with the case. They just went after him on trumped-up charges when they realised they weren't going to get me.'

With ELO past their peak and disbanded, Ozzy now a solo artist managed by Sharon, who he had disowned, and David in prison, an innocent victim of his father's crimes, Don sold off Jet and all its assets to CBS for several million and went into semi-retirement. Professionally battered but personally unbowed, by the time I met him he seemed happy enough with his lot. As he said, 'I still get my suits made at the same tailor's as Frank Sinatra. I still eat a good breakfast everyday.' Other times, he'd tell me little jokes and sing little songs – 'from the old days' when he was a Variety star, headlining the London Palladium. Convinced the book was going to make a fortune, he told me several times, 'This will change your life. And mine,' he'd add cheerfully. The book would give him 'a whole new career, kid. That's my aim.'

He planned to do a one-man show, he said, based on the book – though one didn't see how that might be possible with the Alzheimer's becoming worse, by the end of our time together. There was also talk of his 'son' Harvey Weinstein commissioning a biopic for Miramax – a possibility that seemed more likely – especially when he and David sat me down one day at the pub and began questioning me earnestly about what I 'really wanted' from the book. My deal meant I would have been entitled to 25 per cent of any advance for film rights Don was given but with Miramax talking in the region of $3 million it was clear neither Don nor David was happy with that arrangement any more. David did the soft talking while Don merely sat there staring at me as though he didn't know me suddenly. It was the first – and thankfully the last – time I had ever experienced the Don in negotiating mode. The first time I'd really had an inkling of what it must have been like to deal with the old boy in his terrifying heyday. All for nothing though, as Miramax pulled out of the deal not long after, fazed by an unchaperoned meeting with the old man at which his increasingly frail mental state had set too many alarm bells ringing.

Mostly, though, we had a laugh together. He was fond of berating me for my clothes. I thought I looked smart but casual. He thought I was, 'A fucking disgrace! You look like a ponce. If you're going to hang around with me we're going to have to get you to my tailor's.' And he was always giving me advice on how to conduct myself. 'All that stuff about "sticks and stones" and "words may never hurt me" it's all bollocks,' he told me. 'The thought of violence is much more of a deterrent than the actual deed. By the time you come to actually hurt someone, it's too late for them, it's over. But the *thought* of what you might do to them keeps them right where you want them. Always let your reputation precede you.'

I promised I'd give it a go.

People used to ask me: what's he like? 'He's great,' I'd say. 'I really like him. I'm really glad I didn't know him when he was younger, though.' Things began to get more difficult and much less fun, however, as his Alzheimer's got steadily worse. One of the most distressing symptoms of his disease, I discovered, was the sudden loss of the thread of whatever he was saying. Right in the middle of a sentence his mind would just stop working and not only would he not be able to finish his point, he would forget what it was we'd even been talking about, or why. On such occasions, his mind would invariably revert back to some other story he'd already told me dozens of times, usually what he'd done or was still going to do some old enemy, sometimes now dead, sometimes not. One of his pet hates on such occasions was former CBS Records president Walter Yetnikoff. Yetnikoff had been head honcho at one of the biggest, most powerful record companies in America throughout the eighties – overseeing the careers of everyone from Michael Jackson, to Bob Dylan, Mick Jagger and dozens of other similarly high-profile stars. He and Don's paths had crossed because CBS distributed all Jet's products throughout the period – and because they were very much two peas in a pod when it came to their own cynical view of the music biz. As with so many of Don's long-term business associates, there had eventually been a falling out, details of which no longer seemed to matter so much as what Don planned to do to Yetnikoff one of these fine days 'when I catch up with the fucker.'

Much worse than any threats aimed at Roger Cook or any of the others Don routinely promised me he would one day 'track down and kill,' he reserved a very special place for Yetnikoff in this lexicon of score-settling. I lost count of the times Don – adrift suddenly in the fog of his increasingly distant memories – turned to me and issued the words: 'Have you ever heard of a man called Walter Yetnikoff?' Knowing what was coming, my heart would sink. 'Yes,' I'd say, trying to stop him before he started. 'You've told me all about him, remember?' He would ignore me though and so it would begin. The long diatribe detailing Yetnikoff's many faults; the threat of ultra-violence 'should I ever find him walking down the street where I live or eating in one of my favourite restaurants'; the promise to 'sort that piece of shit out before I die.' It would sometimes be an hour before I could get him off the subject again. Sometimes it was simply impossible and I began to treat the first mention of the dreaded Yetnikoff as the signal that the day's work was over. I would go home on the train with the words, 'Have you ever heard of a man called…' going round and round in my mind.

Despite all this, though, the book began to come together. Often

Don told me his most captivating stories when the tape recorder was turned off and we'd adjourned to the pub for his usual half-pint of lager and some fish and chips. Then I would sit on the train home hurriedly scribbling down as much as I could remember of what he'd just told me. One of these days, it was going to be a hell of a book, I decided. And then something else happened which really did put the kibosh on things, something which neither Don nor Sharon nor anyone else could possibly have predicted: a new 'reality TV' show on MTV called *The Osbournes* which had begun airing in America in February 2002 and overnight became the broadcasting sensation of the year.

At first, it seemed like the incredible success of *The Osbournes* would have a knock-on effect on Don's book, which we had titled *Mr. Big*. David reassured us that Sharon and Ozzy had promised to help promote it. Then, when they flew into London a couple of months later to begin promoting the UK launch of the series, they made a point of taking Don with them on their round of ever more high-flying engagements, most memorably when the old man accompanied them in the televised green room on the *Friday night with Jonathan Ross* show on BBC1. Afterwards, when Jonathan – who had made a disparaging gag on-air about 'the old geezer' sat next to Sharon – learned who the old geezer was, he nearly fell over himself trying to get on Don's good side, getting him to 'promise' he would come on the show as a legitimate guest himself when it was published. Don, who had no idea who Ross was but was still sharp enough to recognise a gift horse when presented with one, beamed and patted Ross's back and promised him he'd be making him 'a special call' one night soon. Oh, how we laughed...

As the weeks and months passed, though, and *The Osbournes* grew so big it became like an out of control rocket no one could control, just hang on for dear life, it was clear that Don's memoirs became less and less important to either Sharon or, more worryingly from my point of view, David. Suddenly, David – who had recently been appointed one of the dozen or more 'assistant producers' on the new talk show Sharon was working on in the US – went from being someone who was on the phone practically every day pushing the whole thing along, to someone who never returned calls, couldn't be reached even by email, and didn't even turn up to see Don very often any more. Sitting in my then office in Baker Street, a short taxi ride from Don's apartment in Park Lane, I was surprised to find myself often the only person checking up on Don on a daily basis. He would ring me sometimes three or four times a day, usually about the book but quite often about something – anything – else. I would go over there and find him in his pyjamas, and make him some tea and toast, only to find the milk had gone off. How long had he been there on his own, I wondered. Not that he ever complained. At least, not about being left on his own to cope. Instead he'd rant at me about something he'd just seen on the TV news, or the noise protesting Palestinians were making at the US Embassy, round the corner from the pub we had gone to in better days.

Eventually Sharon appointed Don a 'minder' – one of her tour managers, Richard Cole – who would be sat in the lounge of the flat whenever I turned up, constantly on the phone talking at the top of his voice, while watching the TV, also turned up to deafening volume. Don, who in his reduced state was finding it hard enough to summon up the memories for our talks, was left completely flummoxed. I could barely hear myself think, so god knows how he was supposed to manage. The situation was grotesque and on those fewer and fewer occasions when David was around I complained. But Cole was Sharon's idea and it soon became clear that David – now drinking deep of *The Osbournes* well himself, including the occasional cameo appearance on the show – was not about to question any decisions made by the Queen Osbourne herself.

It was all rather strange and sad. The stampede to climb aboard the ever-growing gravy train generated by *The Osbournes* I could understand. This, after all, was the business we were all in and if its success helped Don's book take off, then I would be as pleased and delighted as the next court jester. But Don was ill – seriously ill – and getting worse by the day. Where had all the good intentions gone to try and make his last days good ones? If they weren't interested in the book any more, why didn't they just say so?

Foolish, naïve questions. Like her father, Sharon had developed the hugely efficient habit of only turning her attentions to things which mattered to her *right then*. Anything not on her immediate radar weren't so much ignored as simply forgotten about. Things of no immediate consequence for her own situation really did not exist. Until the next time she needed a favour or some such, and then suddenly, like reactivated robots, they all came flashing marvellously back into life. Her abandonment of the Don book really was just par for the course. Where that left Don, though, I had no idea. It was, after all, none of my business, I supposed. It was awfully hard to see it strictly in those terms though on those occasions when he would phone me late at night and start on again about how the book was going to 'change your life, trust me.' Before going into yet another rant about 'the fucking Arabs…'

The last time I saw Don was at Sharon and Ozzy's house in Bucks early in 2003. He had quit the Park Lane apartment and, as he became more ill by the day, was going off to live in the same Hollywood mansion then seen regularly on *The Osbournes*. All that was left was for him to say a few goodbyes but by now he seemed to have trouble remembering who I actually was. Not through any tough-guy act this time, though, but because he really couldn't remember. The thick choking magma of Alzheimer's had descended too far.

I noticed someone I hadn't met before at the house too. A young woman in her late-twenties, not unattractive but dressed very casually in gym pants and trainers, with a young child in tow.

'Who's that?' I whispered to David.

'Don's girlfriend,' he sighed.

I had heard talk of several 'girlfriends' during my time with Don, even answered the phone to one or two. But this was the first I'd actually met. I don't know what happened to her but I presume she never saw the old man again after that day either.

Of course, the story didn't quite end there. When Don's memoirs, *Mr. Big*, were finally published in 2004, Sharon, who I hadn't heard from in over a year, suddenly took umbrage and had one of her business advisors contact Robert, my agent, accusing us of 'taking advantage of a sick old man' and misusing her family name to sell books. Pardon? And yet it was Sharon who had personally asked me to take on the project. Sharon for whom we had arranged a special sneak-peek of the manuscript over a year before publication to check there wasn't anything there she was unduly uncomfortable with. (She did ask for a couple of minor changes which I was happy to make.) Sharon who had told me how she wanted to help her father finish his memoirs before it was 'too late.' Perhaps, then, the book had simply arrived too late? Not for Don perhaps but certainly it seemed for Sharon.

But then as Don himself had told me more than once, 'It ain't about who's right or who's wrong, kid. It's about who wins. And I was always a winner, whatever anyone says about me.' Another lesson his daughter had plainly learned well.

When I learned of Don's death in August 2007 I was strangely moved. I say 'strangely' because I had not seen nor heard from him since that final, painful meeting at Sharon's house in Bucks four years before. And the time I had spent with him was, after all, relatively brief, the best part of a year, no more. Had I known him for longer – certainly had I known him at his scary zenith – I might well have been quietly bidding him good riddance. Had I been able to stay in touch, I no doubt would have seen his passing after such a long illness as a merciful relief. His last years, after all, cannot have been pleasant, hidden away in a nursing home in Hollywood, paid for by Sharon; his enemy for so long now, finally, his one true friend; his precious memories, distorted as they were by ego and one-upmanship, now all gone; his mind, what was left of it, adrift like a bottle, no message inside, on the ocean.

Instead, I was left with my own memories of him, still raging against the dying of the light whenever we met, still singing his silly 'Yiddisher songs' as he called them, still taking the piss out of me and everyone else who ever failed to match up to his own desperately, hypocritically high ideals, still looking for a fight; the eternal rat killer. For all his faults – and who doesn't have those – I had missed him after he was gone and thought of him often. I still do.

He certainly deserved more than the undignified scrap that ensued between Sharon and David, as played out in the tabloid newspapers at the time, over the manner of his funeral. David wanted his father buried alongside his mother at home in England. Sharon had other ideas. There was a falling out. Sharon got her way and David was so furious he vented his spleen by selling his story to the Sunday paper, the *News Of The World*, dishing the dirt on the sister he was relying on for a job just a couple of years before. That's not to take sides. I wasn't privy to whatever went on between the siblings and from my own dealings with him I know David can be as prickly as anyone else in his family. The last time I heard from him, in fact, he rang my office by mistake and when he realised it didn't even bother to introduce himself to my assistant nor pass on any greeting to me, Arden law being that you never knowingly put yourself out for anyone not immediately useful to you.

It was still a shame though that the old man's passing had to be marked by such a sad display of family untogetherness. Some might say the old fart deserved it. Who was it, after all, that taught his children to behave that way? Not me. For the record, I liked Don Arden and I still like Sharon Osbourne. I might even like David again if he'd stop being such a sneak. As another wise old man once sort of said: when you swim with sharks don't be surprised if one of them tries to bite your bollocks off...

Act III
Scene Two:

The Antichrist
Posh & Becks

Because of the success of *The Osbournes*, by now everybody thinks they know something about Ozzy and Sharon Osbourne and the opulently dysfunctional world they shakily preside over. For those of us who had known them for years, however, the success of the show was extremely weird. Ozzy's remark years before about *Spinal Tap* came back to me: 'I didn't think it was funny, I thought it was a fucking documentary, I did!' That's exactly how I felt about *The Osbournes*. Indeed, perhaps the strangest side-effect of the many weird echoes generated by that show was having people that had never actually met either of them telling me what they're really like. Deep down inside, you know? Even my in-laws – both now retired – began referring to 'funny Ozzy' and 'good old Sharon' in the same way they would, say, recalcitrant but immensely loveable relatives from the lucky, struck-it-rich side of the family. Which was disconcerting for someone whose own emotional responses to those

225

names are based around a quite different set of circumstances, from the now almost forgotten days when their fame still centred on Ozzy being the lunatic who bit the head off a bat then tried to murder Sharon. Disconcerting and yet strangely familiar in that so many of the genuinely hilarious things that went on in that show were just like the things that made you laugh out loud so many times over the years. Except you weren't watching it on TV back then. You were just lucky enough to be in the same room. Or unlucky enough. It could depend.

For those people who had never registered the names Ozzy and Sharon Osbourne before, the arrival of *The Osbournes* was a hilarious addition to the TV schedules, pure and simple. Of course, I found it funny too. How could you not when it was full of such water-cooler moments as: Ozzy sitting alone on the sofa struggling with a TV remote control the size of a dinner plate: 'What the fuck am I doing?' he mumbles. 'I'm stuck on the Weather Channel. Jack, Jack, come here and switch this fucking TV on!' Seventeen-year-old Jack enters the picture, an expression of long-suffering stoicism on his face, and shows Ozzy how to change channels. 'I'm a very simple man,' says Ozzy by way of explanation. 'You need computer knowledge to turn this TV on. I pressed a button and the fucking shower came on.' He pauses, then: 'Hey, Jack. Press "blow job".' Or: Ozzy at dinner, unable to hear what his daughter Kelly is trying to say even though she is only a couple of feet away, telling her: 'You've not been standing in front of thirty billion decibels for thirty-five years. Write me a note.' Or in another episode, when Kelly shows Ozzy her first tattoo, a tiny love-heart on her hip, lecturing her earnestly: 'Kelly, you've got that there for the rest of your fucking life' only for him to be seen the next moment showing off the enormous blue dragons he has tattooed across his shoulders and chest. Or the shot of him walking around during Kelly's 17th birthday party yelling 'Don't smoke' while her friends ignore him and dance to some industrial-strength dance-beats. 'What is this?' the Black Sabbath singer and alleged inventor of devil-worshipping heavy metal whines, 'Music to get a brain seizure by?' Or when Jack finds the bayonet for Ozzy's shotgun and Kelly tells them in her trademark spiteful drawl: 'You two are so violent!' To which father and son respond as one: 'Shut up!' Or...

There were so many weird and wonderful moments from the show I could be here all day listing them. Billed as a show about 'the most dysfunctional TV family since the Simpsons', from the moment it was first broadcast in America in March 2002, *The Osbournes* became must-see TV. Launched in Britain and Europe just three months later, by the summer of 2002 *The Osbournes* was a worldwide TV phenomenon, accompanied by the kind of publicity money can't buy. As a result, as I write, here in 2008, Ozzy is approaching his 60th birthday a bigger star now than in all the previous six decades put together. Not only that but Sharon and their children are now global stars too. How did it happen? Why did it happen? In a nutshell, the answer, as with everything good that has happened to Ozzy since he was booted out of Black Sabbath nearly 30 years ago now, can be summed up in one word: Sharon.

'I came back off tour and there was a camera crew in my house,' said Ozzy. 'To be honest, I don't know how it happened...The last thing I wanted was to come home to a camera crew.' That was in October 2001, the crew arriving just in time to catch the family setting up home in their new house, unpacking an entire truckload of broken lamps and vases, Sharon seen promising to 'fucking kill' the recalcitrant removal men with the kind of grim, detached smile of a

Cruella DeVille. The crew stayed until February 2002, by which time it's said they had enough good footage to make three series.

While a large part of the appeal of the show was in seeing someone who was once the idol of disaffected teenagers everywhere – and thus the scourge of all right-thinking parents – transformed into a parent himself, worried his own kids are going to be damned forever for doing…well, the sort of things he did himself for most of his life: take drugs, have sex, copying to the letter the time-honoured phrase he became famous for screaming on stage every night of his performing life: 'Let's go crazy!' But instead of an understandable chorus of 'Now you know how we felt' first America, then everywhere else, took Ozzy to their hearts instead.

Seeing him, hangdog expression clearly visible even behind the blue-tinted spectacles, telling his family: 'I love you with all my heart, but you're all fucking mad!' it resonated with every put-upon mum and dad in the world. That he was Ozzy Osbourne, tattooed millionaire who limped and shook his way across the room to deliver these tirades only added to the appeal. Just like every other dad, his biggest fear was no longer 'going off the rails on a crazy train' as he famously sang on his first solo hit, but lying in bed wide awake at night waiting for the sound of the kids' key in the door. And second to that, the telling-off he endured on a regular basis from 'the old lady' – Sharon. The message that came through with every hilarious episode: they may be rich and live in the kind of gothic Hollywood pile one assumes only Batman does, but they are just like us. As the writer Jon Hotten put it, '*The Osbournes* is fabulous, in part because it runs like the sequel to the *Absolutely Fabulous* joke. Ozzy has been the hedonistic dad, but now he's settled down and grown up.'

And of course, as those of us who have actually known him for years could have told you, there is a vulnerability to Ozzy that makes him even more huggable. Aside from the limp and the shakes, there is the hint of a gut, the signs of deafness, the befuddlement at all that goes on around him. The inability to work the microwave properly, the heavy sigh when Sharon tells him to go and pick up the dog shit from the garden. Unlike all the dozens of copycat shows that have since ensued in its wake, the chief appeal of *The Osbournes* was that it presented its star – Ozzy – as a bumbling incompetent, lovable and all too human. As such it was one of the most extraordinarily revealing programmes ever seen on television. Never mind the endlessly clichéd 'rockumentaries' that told us what we already knew – that rock stars take drugs, fuck willing and far too beautiful girls and get treated like babies by everyone that surrounds them. *The Osbournes* was the first to actually show the banal – yet in Ozzy's case, at least – hilarious truth and, in doing so, actually reveal something important about the human condition, warts and all: Jack and Kelly cringing as mum and dad have a kiss and cuddle – 'Gross,' sneers Kelly; Ozzy first thing in the morning, looking every day of his 53 years, issuing his familiar cry: 'Shaarrooonnnn.'

As Ozzy later said, 'It's all too weird. I'm afraid that people will now hit on the kids for who they are. I sat Jack down the other night and I was telling him not to make new friends now. That the people he meets now, you know, you can never be sure why they might want to befriend you, and he said: "Don't you think I know that, dad?" He knows what's going on.' He went on: 'Since it's been on we've had people trying to get in over my garden wall, trying to see in. I'll be honest with you, I'm finding it all a bit scary. I'm suddenly thinking, what if they kidnap one of the kids or try to steal my dogs?' He pulled his now all-too familiar sad clown's face. 'Everyone's going to me:

"Oh, you're so funny". I'm certainly not trying to be, I'm just me at home most of the time.'

Who was the genius though that realised this would actually work? That name again: Sharon. More than anyone, she could take credit for *The Osbournes*. Living in Beverly Hills next door to Pat Boone, Ozzy had struck up an *Odd Couple*-style friendship over the garden fence with the fifties crooner. Shrewdly noting the comic potential of the situation, Sharon had mooted a possible TV sitcom based on the premise, though not with either the real-life Ozzy or Boone involved, but actors playing facsimiles of their characters. But when scriptwriters sent to work on the idea found the Osbournes' natural humour funnier than anything they might come up with themselves, Sharon went one better and half-jokingly suggested they set the cameras up in the house and just leave them. The result: *The Osbournes* and what turned out to be a supremely apt format for a jaded, post-modern TV world.

Nine months before the first show aired, I had helped Sharon put on a private viewing in London of a film the director Penelope Spheeris had made of the 2000 Ozzfest. Spheeris had previously made the classic *Decline and Fall of Western Civilisation: the Metal Years* (which featured an amusing episode with Ozzy) and the first *Wayne's World* movie. The resultant Ozzfest documentary, *We Sold Our Souls for Rock'n'roll* was both hilarious and shocking and received plaudits when it was aired at the prestigious Sundance festival the same year. Before Sharon could find a mainstream distributor for the movie, though, MTV had agreed to the reality TV format of *The Osbournes*, which essentially picked up where Spheeris left off, losing the music and focusing on the 'reality' behind the scenes. Unfortunately for Penelope, rather like Don's book, once *The Osbournes* took off so spectacularly, all previous projects, including both book and film, were hastily shelved as Sharon began her reinvention, emerging from the rotund caterpillar manager behind the scenes into the pretty butterfly starlet of the actual show, dontcha know.

For while Ozzy forfeited his image as the ne'er-do-well rock star in exchange for TV fame, Sharon now came into her own, from her taste in home décor, a wonderfully lurid combination of mumsy Laura Ashley and gothic skull and crossbones, to the truth about who really wore the trousers in the Osbourne household, the dogs being fussed over while the rock star is ignored. And of course, the tantalising glimpses of Sharon in strict manager mode as Ozzy is pushed from pillar to post, seen backstage on Jay Leno's *Tonight Show*, the tassels on his sweater tangled in the arms of the make-up chair, nearly toppling him over as he tries to stand. 'The next time you come back you'll be talking to him,' says Sharon, referring to Leno. 'Talking to who?' says Ozzy, clearly clueless. 'Jay,' she says, exasperated. 'The next time you come back on the show.' Ozzy's response almost childlike: 'When's that, next week?'

Eventually, of course, the whole family would be back to speak to Leno, such was the phenomenal success of the show, with even the family nanny having her own page on the MTV website. But while dad was seen turning on his 'Ozzy' persona like a factory worker punching the clock, desperate to put his feet up and have a bit of peace and quiet in front of the telly, the depiction of Sharon showed what those of us who know them had realised for some time, that she was not only Beauty to Ozzy's Beast, she was clearly the brains of the team. A powerful woman who had achieved the Cosmo dream – career, marriage, children – and now, the ultimate for this wife and daughter of showbiz: stardom in her own right. It also demonstrated, most touchingly, that despite the outward eccentricity of their relationship, in an industry known for its fickleness, theirs was a lasting partnership, their love all too real.

When, in July 2002, Sharon was diagnosed with colon cancer, I wasn't surprised when she insisted that filming continue. Having literally kicked Ozzy up the arse and pushed him back out on stage countless times over the years when he complained of feeling sick, both mentally and physically, Sharon had proved her trouper credentials many times over. Knowing how shrewd she was, too, one couldn't escape the thought, either, that she would know how much this would also boost interest in both the show and her. Cynical? Not a bit of it. Practical and full of showbiz nous, to the max. Or as Don – who would himself appear in episodes of the second series – knowingly remarked to me at the time, 'She's about to become the new Oprah Winfrey.' Her brother David told me how, shortly after news of her illness became public, he walked into a restaurant in Hollywood with Sharon, 'and the whole place stood up and applauded her.' She also found time during her illness to attend the Creative Arts Emmys award ceremony in LA, accompanied by daughter Kelly, where they received a gong for the Best Reality Television Show award.

Not that Sharon's illness wasn't serious or devastating for those around her. The rest of the family were in pieces. As Ozzy later told me, 'People talk about luck and getting what you deserve. I believe I deserve whatever the man upstairs wants to lay on my plate. Sometimes it's good, sometimes it's not so good. Like when I got the news that Sharon had colon cancer – that fucking did me up, big time. I locked myself away in a room in the dark. At first I couldn't even sleep in the same bed as her cos I was terrified of waking up to her dead body. Then I *would* have been in a fucking mental hospital. Then I got over it and just tried to be with her as much as I could. I'd come home from a show and find this grey little thing in bed. She had several seizures, and every time I'd go to the hospital I'd think, this is it. Not only that, she was opiate allergic. So she could only have ordinary ibuprofen for the pain. But she fought the fucker. She fought back and she won, and I'm so fucking proud of her.'

There was certainly no doubting her courage. As the cancer spread to her lymph glands she was given a one-in-three chance of survival. But she battled on, allowing the MTV cameras to roam freely throughout the house. Ozzy: 'I said to the guy [from MTV], "You want real TV? You can't get any more fucking real than this".' When Sharon's hair fell out during her chemo treatment, she let it be known that she'd had her wigs custom made by Cher's wigmaker. No one was laughing though when it later came out that Jack was suffering from his own drug problems, caused partly by the depression stemming from his mother's condition. When Sharon, the eternal survivor, came out the other end, she did so, she said, 'a stronger, wiser person.' In August 2004, she founded the Sharon Osbourne Colon Cancer Program at Cedars Sinai Hospital, and has continued to speak out on the subject of cancer, which she describes as 'an epidemic.' An honoured guest at the Multiple Myeloma Research Foundation's 2003 Gal, she has also subsequently lent her support to such fundraisers as the Little Tee Campaign for Breast Cancer Care – designing limited edition shirts and vests for them – which donates money for breast cancer research.

Yet it is the aftermath of the show that has proved the more compelling – and strange and funny and tragic – story. Since *The Osbournes*, the real life Osbournes have appeared in all manner of guises, some familiar, some decidedly less so, some utterly bizarre.

While Ozzy has continued to make his own albums, these days adolescent fans empathise more with his teenage kids, Jack and Kelly, than with their weird dad; and while older Ozzy fans might dust off *Diary Of A Madman* or the old Sabbath albums occasionally, few will have cared about his most recent 2007 release, *Black Rain*. Instead, far more attention has been given to one-off recordings like the vocals he contributed, along with former heavyweight champion boxer Frank Bruno and comedian and movie star Billy Connolly, to 'The War Song of the Urpneys' single and album track (although the version heard in the *Dreamstone* movie from which it comes was largely sung by its composer and former Womble Mike Batt); or the special track Ozzy recorded for the *Dog The Bounty Hunter* TV series. And of course, there was his duet with daughter Kelly on the old Sabbath track, 'Changes', which actually reached No. 1 in the UK over the Christmas 2003 holiday period. Less successful but more amusing was his later duet with Miss Piggy of the Muppets on a cover of Steppenwolf's 'Born to Be Wild'. As such, Ozzy's stardom has entered a new, previously unconsidered realm: that of mainstream family entertainer. Some would argue he's not even as famous as his wife any more. Unlike Sharon, though, who now divides audiences into love or hate, Ozzy's shuffling appearance on our screens is still likely to engender feelings of affection. Hence the inductions into various Rock and Roll Halls of Fame, adding his handprints to the Hollywood Walk of Fame, and, most touchingly for him, the Birmingham Walk of Stars on Broad Street, an honour presented to him by the Lord Mayor of Birmingham.

Kelly, meanwhile, has followed her success on TV with her own hit singles and a solo album; part-Buffy, part-Darlene from *Roseanne*, less slick than Britney but more 'street' than a bordello full of Kylies –

again, Kelly now seems likely to become an even bigger TV star. Like her brother, she has had her bouts with drugs and rehab, but unlike contemporaries like Amy Winehouse, she appears to have won her battles and emerged stronger, more opinionated, and certainly slimmer and prettier, than ever. While Jack, of course, has ploughed a more troubled furrow. Speaking to Sharon just before *The Osbournes* took off, she told me she thought Jack had 'all the makings of a real tycoon. He's a brilliant talent spotter, that's why we leave the selection of the Ozzfest bands to him. And yet he's just a teenager.' Since then we've all read the stories about Jack going into rehab and it makes you wonder about the true price for such fame. To the relief of both his mum and dad, however, Jack appears to have worked through his troubles and emerged the strongest, most reliably 'normal' member of the household – or at least the onscreen household. For there is another daughter, of course, the eldest: Aimee. A strikingly beautiful young woman with a voice good enough to encourage genuine aspirations as a singer and enough talent to be considered for a career as a serious actress, she had asked to be excused from the first season of *The Osbournes* (moving into the guest house during filming) because she feared it would impact badly on her budding career, that she wouldn't be taken as seriously afterwards. She may have had a point. But then the success of the show rose to such an unstoppable pitch at its height – dinner at the White House (where President Bush joked: 'Ozzy, Mom loves your stuff'), performing at the Golden Jubilee celebrations of the Queen (singing 'Paranoid', what else?) – that even Aimee eventually acquiesced and agreed to some occasional 'cameo' appearances in the second season. Rumours are now that she is poised to make her big screen debut in a forthcoming movie role.

The biggest star to emerge from *The Osbournes* though has undoubtedly been Sharon. With the rapid success in the nineties of her management company, few realise that she was already a much busier figure in the Osbourne household than her husband and certainly the children, long before *The Osbournes* came along and turned all their worlds upside down. After her initial success with Lita Ford, the Quireboys et al, she went on to even greater commercial reward with acts such as Coal Chamber and the Smashing Pumpkins, before resigning from the latter situation with typically Sharon-like aplomb, announcing 'I must resign due to medical reasons…[singer] Billy Corgan was making me sick!' By then, however, she had become disillusioned with looking after other artists, turning down the chance to oversee the careers of such stars as Guns N' Roses and Courtney Love. Though she didn't know it, she was about to begin work on the most successful artist of her career – herself.

After *The Osbournes*, she was offered her own syndicated daytime talk show in the US, *The Sharon Osbourne Show*, presented as a reflection of her personality and home life, along with the dogs and big double bed in which she would sometimes interview guests such as Elton John. Unfortunately, unlike *The Osbournes*, which presented a fairly accurate portrait of Sharon as the tell-it-like-it-is matriarch of a foulmouthed if funny family, her persona on her own show was far too syrupy, with everyone addressed as 'darling' or 'sweetheart' and her dogs, loveable though they are, receiving far too much airtime. The result was one of the few reverses of her career, the show cancelled after one only moderately successful season.

Luck was smiling on her again though when Simon Cowell had the foresight to offer her a job as one of the judges and mentors on his new UK reality TV talent show *The X Factor*. The show, which began airing on ITV in 2004 to enormous viewer response, has proved to be the making of her, allowing her as it does to be both the ruthless music biz woman she really is and show the softer, more family-oriented side of her personality too, mentoring acts through the various round of the competition. Despite being responsible for some of the most colourful characters that have emerged from the competition, such as Tabby – like a skinny, Panda-eyed former member of the Quireboys – from the first series, 'singing dustman' Andy Abraham and Chico 'It's Chico Time' Slimani from the second, she has never had the winner and her most memorable moment is still probably her live televised outburst against the eventual winner of the first series, Steve Brookstein, on the night of the final show. Afterwards, Brookstein's victory was partly attributed to the fact that Sharon's verbal attack had engendered a large 'sympathy vote' but according to Sharon he was already well ahead at the time. Personally, who won or lost was less interesting than the fact that this was Sharon giving the viewing audience a proper look at what she could really be like when riled. She didn't quite stoop to calling Brookstein a 'dirty motherfucker' but it wasn't far off. Even funnier was when Sharon took part in the spin-off show *The X Factor: Battle of the Stars*, in which she attacked contestant Rebecca Loos, then briefly famous as the former PA who'd had an affair with David Beckham. Now a close 'celebrity friend' of the Beckhams, Sharon left the audience gasping when she told Loos on the first show, 'You should try doing tomorrow's performance with your knickers on because it will help warm up your voice. You have a very bad vibe that comes from you.' A clearly distraught Loos was said to take a great deal of persuading to stay in the competition. But of course she did.

Sharon nearly got herself voted off the programme by Cowell in

2007 after a series of run-ins. Most famously, when Sharon reportedly spoke out against *Who Wants To Be A Millionaire?* presenter Chris Tarrant, who was in the show's audience prior to filming one night during the making of the third series in 2006. Tarrant had made the fatal error of making a joke at Ozzy's expense and Sharon flew to her husband's defence, referring specifically to Tarrant's much-publicised recent infidelity to his wife Ingrid, from whom he was in the process of separating. Cowell was said to have considered giving Sharon her marching orders then but another, even more successful series of *The X Factor* ensued in 2007 with Sharon once again occupying one of the judges' hot seats – joined this time by new face, Dannii Minogue. Sharon caused controversy yet again, however, when she threatened to walk off when two of her three acts were voted off during the first week of the live finals. 'What I did was no good,' Sharon announced, 'and I think I'm going home now,' refusing to take any further part in the show. Naturally, she was back in time for the next episode though.

How much all this stuff is spontaneous and how much contrived, Sharon is far too canny to admit to in public of course but knowing her for as long as I have I'd say it's a fair bet it's mostly contrived with a touch of real anger thrown in too sometimes. Sharon hates to lose and so far she hasn't won any of *The X Factor* competitions. Not on screen anyway. Off screen, however, she has become one of the highest-paid personalities on British television. When she announced in June 2008 that she would be taking no further part in the show, most viewers assumed it was because Cowell had finally wielded the axe. Not so. As shrewd a judge of what makes a hit as Sharon, Cowell has always known the value of a judge that had become even more outspoken than him. In a prepared statement, Sharon's spokesman merely said she 'would like to thank the wonderful British public for their enormous support during what's been an exciting ride. She would also like to take this opportunity to thank Simon Cowell and ITV while wishing them all the best for the next series.'

However, on the eve of the new *X Factor* series starting in August, executive producer Richard Holloway revealed in an interview with the *Sun* that Sharon's departure had partly been down to her 'unreasonable' salary demands. Already on a reported salary of £1.5 million per series, he claimed Sharon had demanded a £500,000 increase for the new series, bringing her salary up to £2 million. He told the *Sun:* 'I think her demands were unreasonable. From a financial point of view, it was absolutely right to say that there was no more money.' Tellingly, however, he added: 'Sharon didn't want to do the next series. We wanted her to stay on, without question, but it was totally and utterly her choice. Pay was part of the situation. ITV couldn't cough up what she was demanding.' And therein lies the rub. Sharon didn't *want* to do the next series, rightly judging the programme had already hit its peak. So in time-honoured managerial style, she simply asked for so much money that she couldn't lose either way. If they refused, as they did, she'd leave a programme she'd already tired of anyway. If they'd given it to her, she'd have stayed on knowing at least she was getting paid a fortune for doing something she no longer wanted to.

But why? Because, as ever, Sharon had bigger fish to fry. Having conceded that fronting her own show was no longer an option – she had tried again unsuccessfully with a British version of the US talk show in 2006, *The Sharon Osbourne Show*, on ITV, but again so-so ratings meant there was only one series – and having tired of the talent show format, despite comparable success to *The X Factor* in the US with her appearances on the second series of *America's Got Talent* – it was recently announced that the whole Osbourne clan was to be reunited onscreen for their own Variety-style show, performing comedy skits and introducing music acts – a bizarre echo of the sort of shows her father used to front over 50 years before. With the series being made by Freemantle-Media – also makers of *The X Factor* and *Britain's Got Talent* – it is tipped to be sold to the US Fox Network, with further deals allowing the show to be aired around the world in 2009. According to a mutual friend, 'It's going to be based on the old *Sonny and Cher Show* in the US from the seventies – with Ozzy being the slow-witted but funny Sonny and Sharon as the smarter, bossy Cher. All in good fun, though.'

How this will pan out remains to be seen. Let's hope it works better than the family's last televised appearance together at the 2008 Brits music awards in London, which was cringe-making, to say the least, Sharon reaching a low point when publicly describing comedian Vic Reeves, who was presenting one of the awards, as a 'piss head' and a 'bastard'. Afterwards, Sharon explained the attack by claiming Reeves was drunk. Reeves denied it, saying he was simply having trouble reading the autocue. Either way, Sharon's vitriolic response was seen as an overreaction at best, an irresponsible performance before a live pre-watershed audience at worst.

Whatever she does next though, neither Sharon nor her family seem able to keep out of the news, whether it be good – a new lucrative contract with the Asda chain; receiving Woman of the Year awards; being offered a role in *The Vagina Monologues* – or bad: losing £2 million worth of jewellery during a burglary at the house in Bucks, including wedding rings, an engagement ring and pearl and diamond necklaces, or fleeing the same house when a blaze threatened to burn the whole place down as it did in 2006. (Fortunately, none of the family was at home.)

When one considers that, according to most recent reports, she and Ozzy are now ranked among the richest people in Britain with an estimated fortune of over £100 million, it seem churlish to criticise their actions. Certainly, her Midas touch doesn't seem to have deserted her when it comes to bestselling books, TV series, albums, concerts and – whisper it – a rumoured forthcoming Osbournes-related film and animation series. Along the way she has not been afraid to show her scars – quite literally in the case of her televised appearance with Dr Phil where she confessed to having had a full rhytidectomy (face lift), abdominoplasty (tummy tuck) and mastopexy (breast enhancement), along with up to a dozen other surgical procedures costing in the region of £300,000, though even she drew the line, she said, at having anything done to her eyes or mouth.

How do you really measure success, though? True success, that is, as opposed to the kind measured by sales figures, ratings, numbers on page? On any objective scale, the success of *The Osbournes* was gargantuan: the most popular show in the 25-year history of MTV, it has subsequently spawned an entire industry and copycat reality TV shows: pop stars seen giving birth on TV; fashion stars seen giving orders to their minions; *Playboy* models seen being, er, *Playboy* models; even rock stars seen giving lessons on how to become rock stars. Plus a whole array of nonentities who have found fame, briefly, before falling away again into the oblivion they first sprung from. None though – repeat: none – has enjoyed the broad, cross-generational popularity of *The Osbournes*. So much so that the ripples – make that waves – are still being felt now, six years and who knows how many belly laughs on.

Yet the real success of the programme, for Sharon and Ozzy Osbourne anyway, can be seen in much smaller, more human ways.

To the public they have become no less than the antichrist Posh and Becks. For Sharon, though, not only has she finally stepped out from the shadows she first occupied as devilish daughter to the Al Capone of Pop, then later as wife to the self-styled Prince Of Darkness, to become a bigger star than either of them, she has also found a certain kind of peace she has never known before. Aided by relentless elective surgery and her own pressing need to reinvent herself for her newfound and largely adoring public, she has lost the weight that made her so self-conscious and full of angst throughout most of her life. Indeed, she looks better now in her mid-fifties than she did in her twenties or thirties. While her husband – long the source of most of her woes as well as her delight – appears finally to have conquered enough of his demons to not turn into the Incredible Hulk the first time someone offers him a drink. A regular attendee of AA meetings, the years of being either off or on the wagon appear to have been replaced by an era of simple acceptance of his plight, and with it a more manageable way of dealing with it. As he told me the last time we spoke in the summer of 2005, 'I don't think about it in terms of being sober or not any more, I just see it as wanting to be happy. And for me being happy means not being drunk or stoned or anything else that is going to freak me or my family out. I just want to be me.'

Not that that means he doesn't get into trouble any more. When, on 8 December 2003, it emerged that he'd been rushed into emergency surgery at Wexham Park Hospital in Slough, following an accident on his quad-bike at home in the grounds of the house in England, it echoed every bizarre incident of his long and incident-filled career. This time, though, the silly sod nearly finished himself off for good, breaking his collarbone, eight ribs, and a neck vertebra. An operation was performed to lift the collarbone, which was believed to be resting on a major artery and interrupting blood flow to the arm, leaving him with two surgical steel bolts in his neck. 'Feel that,' he told me the next time I saw him. Sure enough, it felt like he had something from under a car bonnet inserted beneath his skin. 'Does it hurt?' I asked. 'Only when I shit,' he deadpanned. Sharon later revealed that he had actually stopped breathing before the ambulance arrived and was only saved by his personal bodyguard, Sam Ruston, giving him on-the-spot emergency resuscitation. Not that Ozzy seemed much bothered by any of that now. 'I've given up worrying too much about things,' he said. 'I mean, I still worry like a fuck, but I know now that it don't actually do no good.'

Partly, he explained, this was because he was still undergoing the 12-step AA programme, which encourages straight talking. But that mumbling, cloudy-headed figure we saw in *The Osbournes* was only ever half the story anyway. Behind that stuttering, strangely needy, inadvertently hilarious figure, lurked a far more complex, sensitive individual than his expletive-strewn TV countenance allowed; one that was always taking it in, even when it suited him to act otherwise. And one, most astonishingly, who had now risen Claudius-like to become one of the most famous and fondly regarded people on earth. As he said, 'All my life people treated me like a fucking clown. But who's laughing now, eh?'

What about that visible tremor everybody got used to seeing in *The Osbournes*, was it just the years of drink and drug abuse, or something more? 'Well, I always assumed it was, yeah. Turns out I was wrong. I only just found this out, actually, but it all stems from the family again. A few years ago, I started to develop this really bad tremor. I thought it was from detoxing. I'm thinking, is it the shock? Am I having a nervous breakdown? Now I find out I've got…it's called

243

Parkin, but it's not Parkinson's. Anything to do with the central nervous system, it has the word Parkin in it, apparently. What I've got is called a Parkin hereditary tremor and I have to take medication for it on a daily basis for the rest of my life. When I found out, I phoned my sister, Jean. She goes, "Not you as well!" I said, "What the fuck do you mean, not me as well?" She says, "Oh, mum had that, so did Auntie Elsie and your grandma…" I'm like, "Thanks for fucking telling me!" Me walking around for years thinking I'd got some sort of drug paralysis.'

What was his initial reaction to the success of the show? 'It was like going to bed one night, getting up the next day and opening the door and it's a completely different world out there. I was like, is it me, or is this just really fucking weird? All these TV guys jumping for joy. In the end I asked them, "If the show had been an album, how many records would we have sold?" This guy goes, "You know *Thriller*? Well this is like 18 *Thrillers*". I'm going, *what!?!* Then I was the one jumping for joy!'

And now it was all over, how did he feel about it? 'I'm glad. I'd had enough by the end. One thing I did learn about TV, you think the music business is weird, in TV they really are all fucking mad. I mean, they get up, probably have a bonk or a row, or tread in dog shit or whatever. Then they've got to go on television and go, "HI FOLKS, IT'S JIMMY AND SUE!" They can't go, "Fucking hell, it's raining and I feel like shit…" On a personal level, it's been weird. Like, I just went to an AA meeting. Nobody used to bat an eye when I walked into a meeting, now they all come up to me. It's the same everywhere I go now. People think they *know* me…Meanwhile, suddenly my kids are going off the rails. Jack, at the age of 16, he's doing smack! Then Kelly comes stumbling home one night, trips over and a shit-load of pills come spilling out of her bag. I find out she's been getting them off the Internet! Thank God they're both all right now.'

Had the success of *The Osbournes* helped him become a survivor? 'I don't know about "survivor" so much as blessed or just lucky. I was out there using and abusing for years. I should be dead. They talk about money but, honestly, the most valuable thing to me right now is my sobriety. I've never had this much time to *think* with a clear head. And what I recognise now is that I have certain feelings – certain fears to do with my childhood – that I don't know how to deal with. When I was a kid, we did a lot of shouting but we never communicated big things…Drinking and smoking was normal in our house. When I couldn't sleep my dad would give me a bottle of beer. So for a long time, alcohol was great for me. I loved it and had some great times on it. But then, like everything does, it came to an end. It stopped working, but I still had the fear and the voices in my head telling me to do it.'

Did he still get the voices in his head? 'Yeah. The thing is, it's an illness of the mind, and of the body and the spirit, so you're spiritually sick. And I've got no choice but to accept that, because when I do what's suggested I do, the voices turn down. Cos I used to have a fucking football crowd in my head, you know? Plus, I'm just compulsive. Sharon will ask for a glass of Château De Fuckwit or whatever, but to me it's either red or white and you wake up the next day having pissed the bed. These days I've learned how to turn the voices down. I believe that everything is a balance. You can't have good without bad, you can't have day without night, you can't have light without shade. It's all yin and yang. It's all balance.'

Sharon struck a similar note the last time I spoke to her. It was on the phone. I was talking to Ozzy when she rang and when he told her who he was with she asked to speak to me. It was a few months after her father's book had been published and whatever had been bugging her at the time had all been forgotten, it seemed.

'Darling,' she said. 'How lovely to speak to you! What are you doing? When are you going to bring your lovely wife and children to the house?' The fact that Sharon had never actually met my 'lovely wife and children' hardly mattered. With Sharon, as ever, you were either in or out and if you were in then everything was lovely and always would be.

'I'm fine,' I said, 'How are you?'

'I'm wonderful,' she gushed. 'I've never been happier. Just so busy! Can you believe everything that's happened? The main thing though is that Ozzy's happy and so are the children. I just hope it stays that way…'

After I put the phone down I turned to Ozzy and asked him: 'What's it like for you now that Sharon is also a huge star?' There was a long pause. He exhaled. 'Well, it took a little bit of…readjustment,' he said. 'But I mean, hey, I've got to accept it otherwise it will just drive me mad. I said to her one day, "Fucking hell, Sharon, slow down, darling. You're living as though every day was your last". She says, "You've got that in fucking one!" I thought, okay, shut your mouth, Ozzy, before you get a kick in the bollocks to go with it.'

And you wouldn't want that…

Recommended Reading / Viewing

Books

Diary Of A Madman: The Uncensored Memoirs of Rock's Greatest Rogue by Mick Wall (Zomba Books 1986)

Paranoid: Black Days With Sabbath & Other Horror Stories by Mick Wall (Mainstream Publishing 1999)

The Dirt: Confessions Of The World's Most Notorious Rock Band by Tommy Lee, Mick Mars, Vince Neil and Nikki Sixx with Neil Strauss (Harper Collins 2001)

Ozzy Unauthorised by Sue Crawford (Michael O'Mara Books 2002)

The Osbournes by David Katz and Michael Robin (Andrews McMeel Publishing 2002)

The Osbournes Unauthorised by Reed Tucker (Boxtree Books 2002)

Ordinary People – Our Story by Ozzy and Sharon Osbourne with Todd Gold (Pocket Books 2003)

The Osbournes: Talking by Harry Shaw and Bruce Kavanagh (Omnibus Press 2004)

Mr Big – Ozzy, Sharon and My Life as the Godfather Of Rock by Don Arden with Mick Wall (Robson Books 2004)

Sharon Osbourne: Unauthorised, Uncensored – Understood by Sue Crawford (Michael O'Mara Books 2005)

Extreme: My Autobiography by Sharon Osbourne with Penelope Dening (Time Warner Books 2005)

DVDs

Don't Blame Me: The Tales of Ozzy Osbourne (Epic Music Video 2000)

Mr and Mrs Osbourne – Happy Ever After (IMC Vision 2002)

The Osbournes: Series One (Buena Vista Home Entertainment 2003)

The Osbournes: The Second Series (Buena Vista Home Entertainment 2004)

The Osbournes: Two and a Half (Miramax Entertainment 2004)